D1479277

To

_____

From

_____

Date

_____

To

_____

From

_____

Date

_____

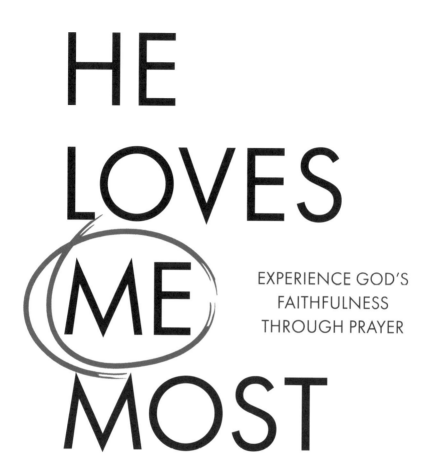

HE LOVES ME MOST

EXPERIENCE GOD'S
FAITHFULNESS
THROUGH PRAYER

. . . .

BROUGHT TO YOU BY
THE WORD FOR YOU TODAY

Press Publishing Group.

HE LOVES ME MOST CHERISHED: EXPERIENCE GOD'S FAITHFULNESS THROUGH PRAYER

International Standard Book Number: 978-1-7923-4821-1

Copyright © 2020 Celebration Enterprises

Roswell, GA 30075
(404) 831-7764

CONTENTS

HEALING

HAVING DONE ALL, STAND IN FAITH WITH PATIENCE

FAMILY

FRIENDS

DIFFICULT RELATIONSHIPS

INTRODUCTION

*P*ut into simplest terms, prayer is the means through which we communicate with God. He has placed into each of us a longing to know and interact with Him. As believers, our response to that longing is facilitated by faith—believing that a relationship with God is possible. The author of the book of Hebrews puts it this way: "Anyone who comes to him must believe that he exists and that he rewards those who earnestly seek him" (Hebrews 11:6 NIV).

God created us so that when we experience something awe-inspiring, we need to offer praise and wrap words around it. This is especially true when we encounter Him! We don't worship God because He needs it, but because we do. Without worship, our perception of Him is incomplete. We forget how great He is; we overlook our calling and become self-involved. When we fail to maintain close contact with Him on a daily basis, we tend to lose our sense of wonder and gratitude. We plod through life with blinders on and become increasingly self-reliant, stubborn, and proud.

Thankfully, prayer grants us the amazing opportunity to know and appreciate God for Who He is, and it positions us to receive countless blessings from His loving hand. Observe these truths about prayer:

1. Prayer is a duty. It's like going to work. You do it because it's a commitment, and because of the rewards it brings.

2. Prayer is a discipline. The old-timers used to talk about "praying through." Through what? Through wandering thoughts, through fatigue, through fears, and every other form of resistance and distraction. When you enter the "prayer zone," Satan will fight you at every turn. But when you stand in the name of Jesus, the powers of darkness will retreat, and you will prevail (See John 14:13-14).

3. Prayer is a delight. If you're faithful to the place of prayer there'll be times when your whole being will be conscious that God is present, answering your prayer, strengthening you, and giving you guidance. The Psalmist said, "When my heart is faint; lead me to the rock that is higher than I" (Psalm 61:2 NAS).

When your resources are depleted and you think you won't survive, God has provided a refuge that's higher than your circumstances—it's the place of prayer where you're under His divine protection and the Enemy has no jurisdiction.

HOW TO GET THE MOST OUT OF
HE LOVES ME MOST

---

*T*his book is not a devotional, though you may choose to study it daily. This book was not created to be a prayer journal, though you will most likely want to make notes of your time in prayer with your Heavenly Father—the ONE WHO LOVES YOU MOST!

Organized by category, dealing with the different seasons and obstacles we all face in life, HE LOVES ME MOST provides you with the building blocks you'll need for an effective and rewarding prayer life that will lead you to a closer relationship with God.

As you make your way through this book, on any given subject, you will find encouraging, biblically sound advice for day-to-day living. You will also find a sample prayer to pray on each topic. And you are provided with a HE LOVES ME MOST statement which is discerned from the content you've studied and the supporting Scriptures.

In addition, we have given you sample **GOD'S PART** text, and sample **MY PART** text on the first three subtopics. We hope that these examples will give you courage to write what you're thinking or feeling. Feel free to add notes to any of these sections within the space provided, or you may choose to use your own journal.

THE ULTIMATE EXAMPLE OF PRAYER

(The Lord's Prayer)

1

HOW JESUS TAUGHT US TO PRAY (1)

"Therefore, pray...Our Father in heaven."

MATTHEW 6:9 NKJV

*H*ere's how Jesus taught us to pray: (1) "Our Father in heaven." When you say, "Father" you are acknowledging that you're "family," that you have a special relationship with God which entitles you to go to Him at any time, confident you're loved, welcomed, and assured of His favor. When you say, "in heaven," you can go no higher. You're drawing what you need from the ultimate source of goodness, grace, mercy, provision, protection, and authority. What a privilege! (2) "Hallowed be Your name" (Matthew 6:9 NKJV). This thought should always be uppermost in your mind: "Whatever I do today, Lord, whether in thought, word or deed, let it honor You." People should be able to look at your life and want to become acquainted with the One you serve. (3) "Your kingdom come. Your will be done on earth as it is in heaven" (Matthew 6:10 NKJV). Each time you choose to say no to yourself and yes to God's will, you demonstrate to a watching world what it means to live as a citizen of His kingdom. Note the words, "as it is in heaven." Is anyone in heaven fearful or doubting? Stubborn or disobedient? Critical or negative? When the enemy brings something to your door that's contrary to God's will, you have the authority to rise up and say, "If it's not done and approved in heaven it has no place in my life here on earth." When it comes to disobedience, refuse to accept the package and sign the receipt. The one thing Satan hopes you never discover is that you have the God-given authority to restrict his movements in your life.

PRAYER

Father, I am so grateful that Jesus provided an example of the right way to pray. Help me to want what You want for my life and not be intimidated when I come before You. Today I ask You to help me develop my prayer life, so that I can talk with You about the things on my heart.

_____

_____

_____

_____

GOD'S PART

Lord, I know that I can't do Your part, and You won't do mine. So I trust you to:

_____

_____

_____

_____

MY PART

[Example] Lord, I realize that I need to stop talking long enough to hear Your voice. I've been talking "at" You, but I want to learn to talk "with" You. Today I choose to stay quiet and listen.

_____

_____

_____

_____

Lord, I know now, that You want to spend time with me. You want to help me grow and gain confidence in my prayer life. And that's how I know, that of all the people in my life, You love me most!

2

HOW JESUS TAUGHT US TO PRAY (2)

"Give us this day our daily bread."

MATTHEW 6:11 NKJV

*J*esus taught us to pray, "Give us this day our daily bread." Notice the word "daily." You can't fight today's battles on the strength of yesterday's bread; you must have a fresh supply. In the wilderness God's people were only permitted to collect enough manna for one day; if they tried to collect more it rotted. It's wonderful to talk about what God did yesterday and what He's going to do tomorrow, but all you've got is today. "Give us this day our daily bread." Only as you partake of what God's provided for you today will you be able to stand up to the challenges you face. This prayer is an expression of faith. The very fact that you ask means you believe God's got what you need and that He cares enough to provide for you. It says, "I don't need to go to anybody else but You, Lord." So, hang up the phone, turn off the TV, shut the door, get down on your knees, approach God in faith and pray, "Give me what I need for this day." God knows what you need, you don't! As you partake of what He provides for you each day you'll be able to handle whatever life throws at you. And one more thought. When people start getting on your nerves for no apparent reason, or you start having all sorts of mood swings, or you begin living by feelings instead of faith, it's probably because you're not eating right. If that's so, it's time to go back to your source and say, "Lord, I've come for my daily bread."

PRAYER

Father, Your Word says that You want to meet my every need. Often, I get in Your way by trying to fix things myself. When I try to rationalize my way out of my problems, I close the door on Your ability to intervene. Help me to recognize Your voice within me, and to do what You direct me to do instead of giving into fear.

_____

_____

_____

_____

GOD'S PART

Lord, I know that I can't do Your part, and You won't do mine. So I trust you to:

_____

_____

_____

_____

MY PART

[Example] Father, the Lord's Prayer is so much more than something I learned as a child. It's Your example for me. I commit to studying the example You gave, and I ask for Your help to turn my ways into Your ways.

_____

_____

_____

_____

> Father, You not only know what I need, but You have already provided a way for me to have my needs met. And that's how I know, that of all the people in my life, You love me most!

3

HOW JESUS TAUGHT
US TO PRAY (3)

"Forgive us our debts as we forgive our debtors."

MATTHEW 6:12 NKJV

*L*et's clear up some misconceptions about the words: "Forgive us our debts, as we forgive our debtors." Satan will try to convince you that if your feelings haven't changed toward the person who wronged you, you haven't truly forgiven them. No, you can make the right decision and still have the wrong feelings! This is when you need faith to carry you through. You have done your part, now you are waiting for God to do His. God has the power to change your feelings toward the one who hurt you, and He will. Another misconception is that all you have to do is make a decision to forgive and then your job's finished. No, you are instructed to "Invoke blessings upon and pray for the happiness of those who curse you, implore God's blessing (favor) upon those who abuse you" (Luke 6:28 AMPC). You say, "Bless them? Are you serious?" Yes. The word "bless" means "to speak well of." You're extending mercy to those who don't deserve it. But isn't that what God does for you? The truth is you cannot truly forgive without the Holy Spirit's help. So today why don't you pray, "Holy Spirit, breathe on me and give me strength. I forgive _____ [name] for what they did. I release them from this debt and ask You to bless them. I turn the situation over to You. I trust You for my total restoration. Help me, Lord. Heal my heart, in Jesus' name, amen." Now, by faith, leave it all in your Father's hands, move forward and anticipate His blessing. You won't be disappointed.

PRAYER

Lord, by an act of my will, I forgive _____ [name] for what they did. I release them and ask You to bless them. I turn the situation over to You. I trust You for my total restoration. Heal my heart, in Your name I pray.

_____

_____

_____

_____

GOD'S PART

Lord, I know that I can't do Your part, and You won't do mine. So I trust you to:

_____

_____

_____

_____

MY PART

[Example] I know I have a blind spot when it comes to unforgiveness. I judge the actions of others based on my own scale of right and wrong, instead of Yours. I know You would never judge me as harshly as I judge others. I really need Your help to become more forgiving. Thank You!

_____

_____

_____

_____

Father, I have held on to this unforgiveness for far too long, but you have given me understanding as to how forgiveness works. And that's how I know, that of all the people in my life, You love me most!

4

HOW JESUS TAUGHT
US TO PRAY (4)

"Deliver us from the evil one."

MATTHEW 6:13 NKJV

Jesus taught us to pray: "Do not lead us into temptation but deliver us from the evil one" (Matthew 6:13 NKJV). Satan knows your areas of weakness and he will exploit them. But there's good news. It's your weaknesses, not your strengths, that draw you closer to God and make you lean on Him. Paul wrote: "I am glad to boast about my weaknesses, so that the power of Christ can work through me" (2 Corinthians 12:9 NLT). At first this verse doesn't seem to make sense. You want to be freed from your weaknesses, not boast about them. But Paul gives you several reasons: (1) Your weakness prevents pride. Paul writes: "So I wouldn't get a big head, I was given the gift of a handicap to keep me in constant touch with my limitations" (2 Corinthians 12:7 MSG). You'll often find a weakness attached to strength, acting as a governor to keep you from becoming boastful or running ahead of God. Gideon chose 32,000 men to fight the Midianites, but God reduced his numbers to 300 (See Judges 7). Why? So that Israel would know it was God's power and not their own that saved them. (2) Your weakness creates fellowship. Your struggles show you how much you need the support of others. Vance Havner said, "Christians, like snowflakes, are frail, but when they stick together, they can stop traffic." (3) Your weakness enables you to help others. It's the broken who become masters at mending. Your most effective ministry can come out of your most painful experiences. The things you're most reluctant to share are often the very things God will use to help others.

PRAYER

Father, I didn't realize that I was being prideful by not recognizing Your desire to come along side of me and make up for my weaknesses. I didn't realize that You want to be strong, when I am not, capable, when I am not, and enough, when I am not.

_____

_____

_____

_____

GOD'S PART

Lord, I know that I can't do Your part, and You won't do mine. So I trust you to:

_____

_____

_____

_____

MY PART

_____

_____

_____

_____

Lord, I know now, that where my abilities end, Yours begin. All I must do is not try to be everything on my own. You make me whole. And that's how I know, that of all the people in my life, You love me most!

5

THE LORD'S PRAYER

"For yours is the Kingdom and the power
and the glory forever. Amen."

MATTHEW 6:13 NKJV

*J*esus points out 3 things we're not built to handle: the kingdom, the power, and the glory. The disciples had no difficulty understanding this. They'd just watched Him calm the worst storm they'd ever been through. In a moment the sea went from a churning torrent to a peaceful pond. Immediate calm! Not even a ripple. And what was their reaction? Listen: "They were in absolute awe, staggered. 'Who is this, anyway?' they asked?" (Mark 4:41 MSG). They'd never met anyone like Him. The waves were His subjects and the winds were His servants. And that's not all; soon they'd see fish jump into the boat, demons dive into pigs, cripples turn into dancers, and corpses become living, breathing people. Never had they experienced such power, never had they seen such glory. Face it, we weren't made to run a kingdom; nor are we expected to be all-powerful. And we certainly can't handle the glory. Some of us think we can. We're self-made. Instead of bowing our knees, we just roll up our sleeves and put in another 12-hour day. Now, that may be enough when it comes to making a living, but when we face our own guilt or our own grave, our own power won't do the trick. So, Jesus ends His great prayer with a message we must never forget: "Thine, not mine, is the kingdom. Thine, not mine, is the power. Thine, not mine is the glory." Remember it—and you'll prosper. Forget it—and you don't want to know!

PRAYER

Father, please forgive me for putting myself on Your level. It wasn't a conscious choice, but one that I allowed to sneak in under the radar. I want to live in all that You have for me, so I humble myself to do it in Your time and by Your direction.

_____

_____

_____

_____

GOD'S PART

Lord, I know that I can't do Your part, and You won't do mine. So I trust you to:

_____

_____

_____

_____

MY PART

_____

_____

_____

_____

> Lord, I am grateful that You love me enough to correct my thinking to align with Your Word. If You didn't care, You wouldn't bother. And that's how I know, that of all the people in my life, You love me most!

6

PERSIST IN PRAYER

"This, then, is how you should pray."

MATTHEW 6:9 NIV

*I*f prayer came naturally, God wouldn't have to remind us so often to do it. A consistent prayer life requires crucifying our selfish nature. But when prayer doesn't seem rewarding, we're apt to abandon it. So how can you pray and get results? (1) Before you ask, adore! Any prayer that begins with asking can become self-centered and shallow. "Enter his gates with thanksgiving and his courts with praise; give thanks to him and praise his name" (Psalm 100:4 NIV). When God's love, goodness and faithfulness are your starting point, you're lifted out of yourself, your spirit is prepared to "connect" with God, the content of your prayer becomes more scriptural, and you get results. In the Lord's Prayer, Jesus directs our attention first to God's name, then His kingdom, then His will. After that, we ask for "our daily bread." Thanksgiving doesn't condition God to bless you—it conditions you to receive His blessing. (2) When you pray, persist! God's not an automated teller. You are supposed to stay engaged with Him until He decides to answer you. This involves an attitude of faith, persistence and patience. Jesus gave us a parable about a woman who kept pleading with a hardhearted judge to grant her petition. When she finally wore him down, he gave her what she asked. Jesus had only one purpose for the parable: "To show them that they should always pray and not give up" (Luke 18:1 NIV). The point is not that persistence forces God's cooperation, it's that God wants you to pray and not quit. When you persist God will answer, "and quickly!" (Luke 18:8 NIV).

PRAYER

Lord, thank you for teaching me how to pray. I used to feel insecure when I came before You. But understanding Your expectations, I have adjusted mine. I don't want to have a distant relationship with You. I am Your child, and You are my Father. I trust You, and I place my life in Your hands.

_____

_____

_____

_____

GOD'S PART

Lord, I know that I can't do Your part, and You won't do mine. So I trust you to:

_____

_____

_____

_____

MY PART

_____

_____

_____

_____

Father, You have thought of everything. You know what I need before I do, and You've prepared a way for me to have my needs met before I even ask. And that's how I know, that of all the people in my life, You love me most!

MAKING PRAYER MY PRIORITY

7

DON'T GET SIDETRACKED

"Everyone is looking for you."

MARK 1:37 NIV

*F*ormer U.S. Secretary of State Henry Kissinger once quipped, "There can't be another crisis. My schedule's already full!" That can happen when other people determine your agenda. Jesus refused to live that way. During His early ministry when word spread about His miracles, "The whole town gathered... and Jesus healed many" (Mark 1:33-34 NIV). The next morning another crowd of needy people was waiting on His doorstep. But how Jesus responded this time might surprise you. "While it was still dark, Jesus...left the house and went off to a solitary place, where he prayed...his companions went to look for him, and when they found him they exclaimed: 'Everyone is looking for you!' Jesus replied, 'Let us go somewhere else...so I can preach there also. That is why I have come'" (Mark 1:35-38 NIV). What was He thinking! There were headlines to be made, people to be healed, and fans waiting to pat him on the back! Could you resist the lure of all that? Jesus did, because He followed God's agenda, not man's. Jesus loved people so much that one day He would die for them. But that didn't stop Him from saying no when He needed to. Appeasing people in order to win their approval is never a good idea; it puts somebody other than God in the driver's seat. Instead of getting sidetracked, Jesus: (a) made prayer and uninterrupted time with His Father a top priority; (b) recognized that doing God's will was more important than "being all things to all people;" (c) refused to let other people's definition of what was urgent, distract Him from fulfilling His life's purpose. So, don't get sidetracked.

PRAYER

Father, please forgive me for putting a thing, a person, or an activity ahead of spending time with You. I want to follow Jesus' example and learn to be okay with disappointing other people. Please heal that place in me that needs to be liked by others.

_____

_____

_____

_____

GOD'S PART

Lord, I know that I can't do Your part, and You won't do mine. So I trust you to:

_____

_____

_____

_____

MY PART

_____

_____

_____

_____

29

He Loves Me Most

Lord, when I give You the reins to my days, I am amazed at what I accomplish. But when I take them back, all the plates I'm spinning fall to the ground and shatter. You have given me an example to follow...all the way to success. And that's how I know, that of all the people in my life, You love me most!

8

MAKE PRAYER A PRIORITY

"We will give ourselves...to prayer and...the word."

ACTS 6:4 NKJV

*I*n Disciplines of a Godly Man, pastor and author R. Kent Hughes says: "Jay Sidlow Baxter once shared a page from his own personal diary with a group of pastors who had inquired about the discipline of prayer. He began telling how...he entered the ministry determined he would be a real man of prayer. However, it wasn't long before his increasing responsibilities, administrative duties, and the subtle subterfuges of pastoral life began to crowd prayer out. Moreover, he began to get used to it, making excuses for himself. Then one morning it all came to a head as he stood over his work-strewn desk and looked at his watch. The voice of the Spirit was calling him to pray. At the same time another velvety voice was telling him to be practical and get his letters answered, and that he ought to face the fact that he wasn't one of the 'spiritual sort'—only a few people could be like that. 'That last remark,' says Baxter, 'hurt like a dagger blade. I couldn't bear to think it was true.' He was horrified by his ability to rationalize away the very ground of his ministerial vitality and power." Understand this: Minutes invested in prayer will give you a greater return than hours spent in ceaseless activity. The New Testament apostles understood that. As the church grew bigger and they became busier, they made a life-changing decision: "We will give ourselves continually to prayer and...the word." As a result, the church grew and multiplied. So, make prayer a priority!

PRAYER
Father, help me to realize that You want me to spend time with You and make You my priority, as I am Yours. Help me to be consistent and committed in my time with You.

_____
_____
_____
_____

GOD'S PART
Lord, I know that I can't do Your part, and You won't do mine. So I trust you to:

_____
_____
_____
_____

MY PART

_____
_____
_____
_____

31

Lord, thank you for being patient with me on this journey, and for helping me see how important it is to put You first in my life. And that's how I know, that of all the people in my life, You love me most!

9

MAKE PRAYER A HABIT

"He knelt down...three times [a] day, and prayed."

DANIEL 6:10 NKJV

*P*eter, whom God used to help build the church, and John, whom God used to write the book of Revelation, made time in their daily schedule for prayer. "Peter and John went up together to the temple at the hour of prayer, the ninth hour" (Acts 3:1 NKJV). The apostle Paul, who wrote much of the New Testament, said, "Never stop praying" (1 Thessalonians 5:17 NLT). Daniel's habit of praying was so well-known that his enemies used it to trap him. "He knelt down on his knees three times [a] day, and prayed and gave thanks before his God, as was his custom since early days. Then these men assembled and found Daniel praying" (Daniel 6:10-11 NKJV). End of story? No, Daniel's prayers shut the mouths of lions and caused a heathen king to say: "'Men must tremble and fear before the God of Daniel. For He is the living God...His kingdom is the one which shall not be destroyed...He delivers and rescues, and He works signs and wonders in heaven and on earth, Who has delivered Daniel from the power of the lions.' So...Daniel prospered" (Daniel 6:26-28 NKJV). The Psalmist wrote, "He who dwells in the secret place of the Most High shall abide under the shadow of the Almighty" (Psalm 91:1 NKJV). Once you identify your "secret place" and begin to use it regularly, a kind of aura surrounds it. You will grow to love it, and eventually it will become the most important place in your life. The power of prayer defies calculation. Nothing lies beyond the reach of prayer, except that which lies outside the will of God.

PRAYER

Lord, I now see why You want me to make prayer a habit. It's never come naturally to me because I haven't made spending time talking with You in prayer a priority. Help me do better so that I grow to love spending time with You.

_____
_____
_____
_____

GOD'S PART

Lord, I know that I can't do Your part, and You won't do mine. So I trust you to:

_____
_____
_____
_____

MY PART

_____
_____
_____
_____

> Father, I am starting to understand just how much You want to spend time with me. I am starting to see things through the lens of Your Word. And that's how I know, that of all the people in my life, You love me most!

10

SIMPLE, BELIEVING PRAYER!

"You can pray for anything, and if you believe...it's yours."

MARK 11:24 TLB

*E*very failure is, in essence, a prayer failure! Think about that. If you don't pray, the best thing that can happen—is nothing. You see, prayer puts the situation into God's hands, otherwise whose hands is it in? But it's useless to pray if you have; (a) no faith that God will answer; (b) no confidence because you feel too unworthy; (c) you think that prayer is about...the right words... the right feeling...the right posture...or the right length of time. Sometimes we say, "I'll remember that in my prayer time." No, you can pray anytime anywhere, about anything (Ephesians 6:18 KJV)! Your prayers can be verbal or silent, long or short, public or private. The verse, "Pray without ceasing," just means—be in conscious contact with God at all times. You say, "But I don't feel like my prayers are good enough to get an answer." Then there are two things you need to know: First, The Spirit helps you in prayer. Listen, "He does our praying in and for us...and keeps us present before God" (Romans 8:26-27 MSG). Second, Jesus stands continually before God on your behalf. Listen again, "He lives forever to plead with God on [our] behalf" (Hebrews 7: 25 NLT). Now, if two out of the three persons in the Godhead are working for you, surely even the most imperfect prayer, will be perfected by the time it arrives at the Throne of God! Knowing that should take the pressure off, and help you develop confidence in simple, believing prayer!

PRAYER

Father, I have heard people pray in many ways. I'm not sure which way is right or which way is wrong. Prayer has always seemed intimidating to me. Thank you for showing me how simple it is to have a conversation with You.

_____

_____

_____

_____

GOD'S PART

Lord, I know that I can't do Your part, and You won't do mine. So I trust you to:

_____

_____

_____

_____

MY PART

_____

_____

_____

_____

35

Lord, I am so afraid that I will do it the wrong way, that often, I don't pray at all. But Your love has pursued me, and You have given me the perfect example of prayer in Your Word. And that's how I know, that of all the people in my life, You love me most!

HOW TO PRAY WITH CONFIDENCE

11

"GOD IS ABLE"

"Being fully convinced that what He had
promised He was also able to perform."

ROMANS 4:21 NKJV

The reason we don't turn to God more often is because at some basic and unconscious level we are not "fully convinced" He is able and willing to move on our behalf. Being able to admit that to yourself is humbling; it's also the point at which you begin to deal with your lack of faith in God. Nothing in your life will change until you pray, "Lord, help me. I say things with my lips that I don't follow through in my behavior." Once you begin to pray that way you can start walking through your Bible, rediscovering that "God is able." He's able to provide for you when you're in a wilderness. He's able to defeat the giants that stand in your way. He's able to go through fiery trials with you and bring you out unharmed. He's able to promote you when you've been overlooked or opposed. "Now to Him who is able to do exceedingly abundantly above all that we ask or think, according to the power that works in us" (Ephesians 3:20 NKJV). Whatever it takes to own the words, "God is able," do it; otherwise you won't be able to pray with confidence. You'll make a few wishes on your knees, but you won't be able to persevere in prayer until you know in your heart of hearts that God is able—and that He's willing! Nothing is too difficult for Him. He's just waiting for you to recognize that and come to Him in faith asking for help.

PRAYER

Father, there are times when I have something important I need to pray about, but I don't come to You because I am not convinced You will hear me. Help me grow in confidence before You, so I can be sure that You hear me and that You are willing to answer my prayers.

_____

_____

_____

_____

GOD'S PART

Lord, I know that I can't do Your part, and You won't do mine. So I trust you to:

_____

_____

_____

_____

39

MY PART

_____

_____

_____

_____

Lord, today I know that You are able, and You can make a way for me no matter what I am facing. And that's how I know, that of all the people in my life, You love me most!

12

CONFIDENCE BEFORE GOD

"Your sins are forgiven."

MATTHEW 9:2 NASB

*J*esus said to a quadriplegic lying on a cot, "Take courage, son; your sins are forgiven." Perhaps you're asking, "What sins could a quadriplegic commit?" There are three ways to sin: (1) Commission: the things we do. (2) Omission: the good we fail to do. (3) Disposition: our wrong attitudes. Why didn't Jesus just say, "Arise, take up your bed and walk?" Because when you know that your sins are forgiven you have the confidence to ask God for what you need, and the courage to rise up in faith and do what He tells you. Knowing his sins were forgiven enabled this man to do what everybody thought was impossible. There's an important lesson here. After Adam sinned, he hid from God. When God said to him, "Where are you?" he replied, "I heard Your voice in the garden, and I was afraid" (Genesis 3:9-10 NKJV). How can you know when something is wrong for you? When it causes you to hide from God! When it makes you avoid prayer, Bible reading, and fellowship with God's people. The Bible condemns sins such as stealing and lusting, but what about other things that are not so clearly spelled out in Scripture? To know whether something is right or wrong for you, you need only ask one question: "How will this affect my confidence before God?" You'll never go wrong asking that question. "If our heart does not condemn us, we have confidence toward God. And whatever we ask we receive from Him, because we keep His commandments and do those things that are pleasing in His sight" (1 John 3:21-22 NKJV).

PRAYER

Lord, when I read, "If our heart does not condemn us, we have confidence toward God. And whatever we ask we receive from Him." I recognize my habit of avoiding You when I blow it. Please forgive me. And help me to run TO You not away FROM You.

_____

_____

_____

_____

GOD'S PART

Lord, I know that I can't do Your part, and You won't do mine. So I trust you to:

_____

_____

_____

_____

MY PART

_____

_____

_____

_____

41

Like a child hides from a parent when they do something wrong, I find reasons to skip my prayer time because I know I've sinned. Your Word says that You are quick to forgive when I confess my sins. And, that's how I know, that of all the people in my life, You love me most!

13

ALL THE GRACE WE NEED

"Let us draw near with confidence to the throne of grace."

HEBREWS 4:16 NASB

*H*ebrews 4:16 says we can "draw near with confidence to the throne of grace." We don't have to hold anything back in prayer. And we don't have to wonder if we are wasting our time. We have been authorized to enter His throne room, using the name of Jesus. Aren't you glad it's not a throne of judgment? Who among us could stand it? No, it's a throne of grace, "unmerited favor." It's a throne because the One who sits on it is the Sovereign Ruler of the universe. It's also where our Father gives His sons and daughters what we could never give ourselves. Yes, He gives us what we don't deserve and could never earn, from a throne that never runs low in its provision—and it is all tied to our drawing near in prayer. God has all the grace we need to help us, but we must go before His throne to ask for it. Therefore, a prayer-less Christian is also a grace-less Christian! Christians who are not praying as a way of life are not growing in their spiritual life because they are not hanging around the throne that dispenses grace. Notice, the grace we receive at God's throne is designed to help us "in time of need." Think about that. Grace is given based on the need of the moment. God will not give you tomorrow's grace until tomorrow, so don't bother asking for it. But don't worry, the provision of grace we have in Christ will not run out tomorrow, or ever. So, you can't go to God too often!

PRAYER

Father, thank you that I do not have to hold anything back from You, and that I can come to your throne of grace anytime I need to, confident I will receive Your grace and favor.

_____
_____
_____
_____

GOD'S PART

Lord, I know that I can't do Your part, and You won't do mine. So I trust you to:

_____
_____
_____
_____

MY PART

_____
_____
_____
_____

Your patience with me is unending. I don't fully understand how You can put up with how long it takes me to make changes in my life. Yet, you wrap me in Your grace. And that's how I know, that of all the people in my life, You love me most!

14

KEEP IT SIMPLE

"They think they will be heard because of their many words."

MATTHEW 6:7 NIV

One Christian author writes: "The purpose of prayer is to release our faith—not repeat phrases over and over. For example, if I need forgiveness I can pray: 'Lord, I lost my temper and I'm sorry. By faith I receive your forgiveness, Amen.' Or I can pray: 'Lord, I'm so wretched. I can't seem to do anything right. No matter how hard I try I'm always screwing up. I don't know what I'm going to do—I've got to stop getting mad. Please forgive me. I'll never do it again. I feel so guilty, so bad; I don't see how you can use me. Well Lord I don't feel much better, but I'll try to believe I'm forgiven.' You'll agree that the first prayer is much more effective than the second." Then, she continues: "My problem was, I didn't have faith that my prayer would get through if it was simple, short and to the point. I'd fallen into the trap of the-longer-the-better. Most of the time I felt confused and unsure, as though I still hadn't gotten the job done. But not anymore. Now I 'keep it simple' and I experience a much greater release of faith, plus I've confidence that God has heard and will answer." Be honest with yourself about your prayer life and make adjustments. If you're not praying enough, pray more. If your prayers are too complicated, simplify them. If you need to keep them more of a secret, quit talking about them to everybody you meet. In other words—keep it simple!

PRAYER

Lord, I've really struggled with keeping my prayers simple and to the point. Sometimes I say too much, and other times I think I've missed the mark by not sharing more details. I will go back and study how Jesus' prayed, so that I can have a more effective prayer life.

_____

_____

_____

_____

GOD'S PART

Lord, I know that I can't do Your part, and You won't do mine. So I trust you to:

_____

_____

_____

_____

MY PART

_____

_____

_____

_____

> Father, there are times when I am so lost for words, that all I can do is speak the name of Jesus. Someone once said that it's like throwing the whole Bible at my problem. It works! And that's how I know, that of all the people in my life, You love me most!

15

YOU MUST EXERCISE FAITH

"He couldn't do any miracles among them...
And he was amazed at their unbelief."

MARK 6:5-6 NLT

*G*od answers prayer in a manner directly related to our level of faith. "According to your faith be it unto you" (Matthew 9:29). Yet sometimes despite our doubts and human reasoning, He comes through for us anyway. The believers praying for Peter's release from prison were amazed when he suddenly appeared on their doorstep (See Acts 12). When Jesus returned to His hometown and began to teach in the local synagogue, the people were amazed by His wisdom. Because He lacked formal education and Ivy League credentials, they wrote Him off as "just a carpenter" (Mark 6:3 NLT). And the result? "Because of their unbelief, he couldn't do any miracles among them except to place his hands on a few sick people and heal them." Question: How often does your unbelief tie God's hands? The truth is: (a) sometimes our faith is so weak that we don't expect Him to answer at all; (b) we fail to pray with confidence; (c) we don't prepare ourselves for what He wants to do for us. You can't ask God for forgiveness, then continue to live under condemnation over sins He has put under the blood. Or pray about your financial situation, then worry yourself sick about how He's going to meet your needs. You can choose to live by your feelings, or in a way that reflects total trust in God. The Bible says, "Without faith it is impossible to please Him, for he who comes to God must believe that He...is a rewarder" (Hebrews 11:6 NKJV). So, you must exercise faith.

PRAYER

Lord, I never realized that I have such an important part to play in getting my prayers answered. I've been leaving all the heavy lifting to You. So today, I make a change. I am going to trust that what You say in Your Word is true, and I am going to believe that my prayers are already being answered.

_____
_____
_____
_____

GOD'S PART

Lord, I know that I can't do Your part, and You won't do mine. So I trust you to:

_____
_____
_____
_____

MY PART

_____
_____
_____
_____

Father, I realize I've been making the whole process of prayer too complicated, and I've ignored my part in getting my prayers answered. Yet, You show me in Your Word there is hope for me. And that's how I know, that of all the people in my life, You love me most!

UNDERSTAND THAT GOD IS EAGER TO ANSWER MY PRAYER

16

KEYS TO ANSWERED PRAYER

"I waited patiently for the Lord to help me..."

PSALM 40:1 NLT

*A*re you waiting for God to move on your behalf? If so, here are some keys. First remember, faith alone qualifies you to receive. It separates you from those who need, and places you among those who receive. David made his expectations known. He talked like a man who expected only the best from God. Whether you know it or not, your words are deciding what your tomorrow will be like. Everything you say either brings you one step closer or pushes you one step further away from what God's promised you. Do you need to break a life-time habit of negative thinking, and doubt-filled words? If God says it, that settles it! Listen, "...For I will hasten my word to perform it" (Jeremiah 1:12 KJV). You are the creation, and He is the creator. Stop trying to out-think the One who made you. Instead feed your faith, for if you don't, it will die. Next, constantly create a climate where doubt and fear can't survive! Atmosphere matters. You can't grow bananas in Alaska. The climate is wrong. But in a climate of praise your faith will begin to work. When King Saul was depressed, David worshiped on his harp and the spirit of depression left him immediately. (See 1 Samuel 16:23 KJV). Anointed music always creates a climate which builds you up and enables God to move—so why don't you give it place in your life? That's another key to answered prayer—use it.

PRAYER

Father, I understand my words play a huge part in getting my prayers answered. I will be more conscious about not giving into negative thinking and doubt-filled words. I will keep the climate of my heart right and I will remember to praise You before I ask for anything.

_____
_____
_____
_____

GOD'S PART

Lord, I know that I can't do Your part, and You won't do mine. So I trust you to:

_____
_____
_____
_____

MY PART

_____
_____
_____
_____

I know that You hear me and that You want to answer my prayers. Thank you for reminding me how important it is to thank you before the answer even comes. And that's how I know, that of all the people in my life, You love me most!

17

DON'T BE AFRAID, PUT GOD FIRST

"I have commanded a widow...to provide for you."

1 KINGS 17:9 NKJV

When famine hit Israel, God said to the prophet Elijah, "Go to Zarephath...I have commanded a widow there to provide for you." Observe three things in this story: (1) When the need arises, your provision will be in place. That's how God works, so ask Him to tell you where to go and what to do. And when He does, get moving! (2) The people God uses will surprise you. Sometimes they're people you would tend to overlook. This penniless widow had "only a handful of flour...and a little oil" (1 Kings 17:12 NKJV). That's no problem to God. He doesn't need much to start with in order to do something great, just a willing heart. Why didn't God send Elijah to a wealthy family? Because they didn't need a miracle, she did. When God's work has a need He looks for someone with a seed, stretches their faith, and both the giver and God's work are blessed. (3) Your "bad time" is often God's opportune moment. This miracle took place in the middle of an economic depression. What seems like the worst possible time for you, is when God loves to move. This woman was only one meal away from death; it doesn't get much worse. "So, she went away and did according to the word of Elijah...she and...her household ate for many days. The bin of flour was not used up, nor did the jar of oil run dry" (1 Kings 17:15-16 NKJV). The key to her miracle is found in Elijah's words: "Do not fear...but make me a small cake from it first" (1 Kings 17:13 NKJV). The Word for you today is: Don't be afraid; put God first and He will meet your need.

PRAYER

Lord, your process for answering prayers makes perfect sense. I will be careful to make sure I hear from you first, and not try to figure out what to do on my own. I want to sow seed, where and when You tell me to sow it. And then, I can expect my harvest in due season.

GOD'S PART

Lord, I know that I can't do Your part, and You won't do mine. So I trust you to:

MY PART

Father, Your Word says that you know what I need before I even ask. And You also make a way to answer my prayer. And that's how I know, that of all the people in my life, You love me most!

18

SPIRITUAL LANDMARKS

"This I call to mind and therefore I have hope."

LAMENTATIONS 3:21 NIV

*Y*ou need to establish some spiritual landmarks in your life to remind you of the times when God intervened on your behalf. Someone said, "We're not slow learners, just quick forgetters." How soon we forget or claim credit for things we had little to do with. When God parted the Jordan River for His people to cross over, He knew something they didn't—that on the other side they would face some big challenges, including the City of Jericho. That's when they would need "reminders." So, He told them to collect twelve stones from the Jordan and build a monument, so they and their children would recall His past faithfulness to them. Samuel did the same after Israel defeated the Philistines. He took a stone and named it Ebenezer, meaning, "Thus far the Lord has helped us" (1 Samuel 7:12 NKJV). Before you give in to discouragement, doubt, or defeat, stop and recall what God has done for you "thus far." Like the day you met Jesus, or the times He guided you, or the doors He opened that you thought were permanently shut, or the scrapes He brought you through. Keep a record of these events and refer to it often. It will help you to remember His goodness when you tend to forget it. It will give you a sense of gratitude for yesterday's blessings, and confidence to face whatever tomorrow brings. "This I call to mind and therefore I have hope: because of the Lord's great love we are not consumed, for his compassions never fail. They are new every morning; great is your faithfulness" (Lamentations 3:21-23 NIV).

PRAYER

Father, I am going to make it a point to stop and remind myself of Your faithfulness toward me. I will recall your goodness in my life and all the times You've shown up for me. I am grateful that Your Word says, You never change.

_____

_____

_____

_____

GOD'S PART

Lord, I know that I can't do Your part, and You won't do mine. So I trust you to:

_____

_____

_____

_____

MY PART

_____

_____

_____

_____

Lord, it's so easy to get caught up in what I'm going through today, that I don't look back at what You've already done for me. Your track record is perfect. And that's how I know, that of all the people in my life, You love me most!

19

THE IMPORTANCE OF YOUR SELF-TALK

"This I recall to my mind; therefore, I have hope."

LAMENTATIONS 3:21 NASB

*L*amentations chapter three describes how despair can engulf us, and how we can conquer it. Jeremiah's downward spiral starts in verse one: "I am the man who has seen affliction" (Lamentations 3:1 NASB), and morphs into an unhealthy preoccupation with his troubles. When our circumstances deteriorate, our self-talk sounds a lot like Jeremiah's. He blamed God for his physical symptoms, his emotional anguish, and his sense of entrapment. He rehearsed God's failure to answer his prayers, and his fear that he'd been singled out as an object of public ridicule: all classic elements of depression. No wonder he felt hopeless! (See Lamentations 3:18). That kind of self-talk can intensify despair and depression and feed our negative outlook. The turning point came when Jeremiah changed his self-talk: "This I recall to my mind; therefore, I have hope." He changed his thought process by recalling God's goodness and mercy: "Because of the Lord's great love we are not consumed for his compassions never fail. They are new every morning; great is your faithfulness" (Lamentations 3:22-23 NIV). When you change your mind—you change your mood! It doesn't happen automatically; you must deliberately refocus your thinking when you least feel like doing it. Notice: Jeremiah's circumstances didn't improve—his outlook did. A stream of encouraging thoughts triggered a change in his self-talk: "'The Lord is my portion'…'therefore I have hope in Him'" (Lamentations 3:24 NASB). That's how important your self-talk is!

PRAYER

Father, I'm glad that You are the only One Who hears the thoughts that run through my head. You probably wonder if I'm ever going to see myself as You see me. Today, I make a conscious decision to catch myself mid-sentence and choose to see myself through Your eyes.

_____
_____
_____
_____

GOD'S PART

Lord, I know that I can't do Your part, and You won't do mine. So I trust you to:

_____
_____
_____
_____

MY PART

_____
_____
_____
_____

Once I make the conscious decision to see myself as God sees me, my confidence will grow, because no one knows me like You. And that's how I know, that of all the people in my life, You love me most!

20

GOD ANSWERS PRAYER

"He will call upon me, and I will answer him..."

PSALM 91:15 NIV

*I*n the summer of 1876, grasshoppers nearly destroyed all the crops in Minnesota. The following spring, farmers were worried that the plague would come back again and bring financial ruin to the state. The situation got so serious, that Governor Pillsbury proclaimed a day of prayer and fasting. All the schools, stores, and offices closed, and men, women, and children, gathered to pray. The next day temperatures soared to mid-summer levels, even though it was only April. Suddenly they were devastated to discover billions of grasshopper larvae, wriggling to life. For three days the unusual heat persisted, and the larvae hatched. It appeared it wouldn't be long before they started feeding, which meant they'd again destroy the state's entire wheat crop. But on the fourth day, the temperature suddenly dropped, and a heavy frost covered the earth killing every one of those creeping, crawling pests, just as surely as if poison or fire had been used. Grateful farmers never forgot that day. It went down in the history of Minnesota, as the day God answered the prayers of the people. It's time we re-discovered the power of prayer. When you pray, you're not overcoming God's reluctance, you're just discovering His willingness. Listen to what He says, "...call on me and I will answer..." (Psalm 91:15 KJV). Why don't you do it?

PRAYER

Lord, so often I try to figure out how You're going to answer my prayer and when I don't see it coming to pass as I envisioned, I allow myself to lose hope. You have millions of ways to answer my prayers. Forgive me for looking in the wrong places, when I should be patiently waiting—in faith—for Your way.

_____

_____

_____

_____

GOD'S PART

Lord, I know that I can't do Your part, and You won't do mine. So I trust you to:

_____

_____

_____

_____

MY PART

_____

_____

_____

_____

> You know what I need before I ask. If I acknowledge You first in all I do, You will direct my path. And that's how I know, of all the people in my life, You love me most!

HOPE

21

HOPE

"Let us hold tightly without wavering to the hope."

*S*ome of the people around you today are living without hope. Look at them; they smile, but their eyes are dead. They talk, but the music has left their voice. They're like mannequins: all dressed up and going nowhere because they feel hopeless. But as a follower of Christ, you don't have to live that way. "Let us hold tightly without wavering to the hope we affirm, for God can be trusted to keep his promise." Our hope isn't luck, like winning the lottery. No, it's confidence that God will do what He said. No one knew the truth of this better than David. He had every reason to lose hope. After Samuel anointed him to be Israel's next king, he had to wait for seven years while a paranoid ruler occupied the throne. He had to flee for his life and hide in caves surrounded by enemies. He saw Israel devastated, his friends killed, and his family taken captive. But he never wavered or threw in the towel. Faced with circumstances that would wipe many of us out, the Psalmist said, "My hope is in You" (Psalm 39:7 NKJV). "Weeping may endure for a night, but joy comes in the morning" (Psalm 30:5 NKJV). In other words, "It's going to get better!" You can't lose with an attitude like that. David became king because he never lost confidence in the promises of God. They kept him focused; they kept him on top of the circumstances; they kept him going! What has God promised you? Stand on His Word and declare, "If God promised it, I believe it, and that settles it!"

PRAYER

Lord, I'm looking everywhere but at You to help me through what I am facing. Your Word says that hope is the step before faith. It can't be seen with my eyes, so I must start looking at what Your Word says about what I'm going through and not waiver or give up hope.

_____

_____

_____

_____

GOD'S PART

Lord, I know that I can't do Your part, and You won't do mine. So I trust you to:

_____

_____

_____

_____

MY PART

_____

_____

_____

_____

Hope is not something that comes out of thin air.
Real hope is born through my trust in God, His Word,
and His track record. And that's how I know, that
of all the people in my life, You love me most!

22

WORDS TO LIVE BY IN TROUBLED TIMES

"The word of our God stands forever."

ISAIAH 40:8 NKJV

*H*ere are some more wonderful promises from the Bible that you can stand on when trouble comes: (1) "Because you have made the Lord...your dwelling place, no evil shall befall you, nor shall any plague come near your dwelling; for He shall give His angels charge over you, to keep you in all your ways" (Psalm 91:9-11 NKJV). (2) "The angel of the Lord encamps around those who fear him, and he delivers them" (Psalm 34:7 NIV). (3) "I will take refuge in the shadow of your wings until the disaster has passed" (Psalm 57:1 NIV). (4) "The Lord is close to the bro-kenhearted and saves those who are crushed in spirit" (Psalm 34:18 NIV). (5) "The eyes of the Lord are on the righteous and his ears are attentive to their prayer" (1 Peter 3:12 NIV). (6) "He reached down from on high and took hold of me; he drew me out of deep waters. He rescued me from my powerful enemy, from my foes, who were too strong for me...he rescued me because he delighted in me" (Psalm 18:16-19 NIV). (7) "Do not gloat over me, my enemy! Though I have fallen, I will rise. Though I sit in darkness, the Lord will be my light" (Micah 7:8 NIV). (8) "You will have courage because you will have hope. You will take your time and rest in safety. You will lie down unafraid, and many will look to you for help" (Job 11:18-19 TLB). (9) "Now to him who is able to do immeasurably more than all we ask or imagine, according to his power that is at work within us" (Ephesians 3:20 NIV).

PRAYER

Father, I am learning to pray the way You want me to pray, and I'm starting to have more confidence in my relationship with You. I'm not afraid that I'm wasting Your time anymore. And the best part is, I am learning to not let anything I see or hear sway me from standing on Your Word.

GOD'S PART

Lord, I know that I can't do Your part, and You won't do mine. So I trust you to:

MY PART

I'm changing my bad habit of spending too much time fixated on my problems. Instead, I am keeping Your Words in front of me and I'm holding them close to my heart. And that's how I know, that of all the people in my life, You love me most!

23

KEEP YOUR HOPE ALIVE

"Having hope will give you courage you will
be protected and rest in safety."

JOB 11:18 NLT

*H*ope is a powerful force. It arouses your mind to explore every possible angle. It enables you to overcome the daunting obstacles. It's absolutely essential to the life God wants you to live. It's the fuel your heart runs on. It's the single biggest difference between those who persevere and those who give up. Hope is what makes couples say, "I do," without any guarantees, and later, after all the broken promises, pick up the pieces and try again knowing it can get better. It's why composers agonize over a score and artists over a canvas, believing some glimmer of beauty will emerge from the struggle. As an old man Henri Matisse was crippled with agonizing arthritis. When asked why he continued to wrap his swollen fingers around a brush every day he replied, "The pain goes away; the beauty endures." Laboring to paint the ceiling of the Sistine Chapel, Michelangelo grew so discouraged that he wanted to quit. But every morning hope pushed him up the ladder to fulfill his magnificent vision. Hope is what made Abraham leave home without knowing where God was taking him. It made Paul challenge the powers of Rome. It's what fueled the Old Testament prophets to keep taking on City Hall! This is not blind optimism, but faith focused, and hope—in God. "You have been my hope...my confidence since my youth" (Psalm 71:5 NIV). You can survive the loss of many things, but not the loss of hope. Nobody experienced greater loss than Job, yet he wrote: "Having hope will give you courage." So, keep your hope alive by trusting in God!

PRAYER

Lord, I ask you today to teach me how to keep stoking the fire of hope in my heart. I know that having hope will give me courage, but it's the in between stage of my asking and Your answering that I need help with. I am determined to not let it slip away.

_____

_____

_____

_____

GOD'S PART

Lord, I know that I can't do Your part, and You won't do mine. So I trust you to:

_____

_____

_____

_____

MY PART

_____

_____

_____

_____

> Hope is more than a word—it is essential to the life You want me to live. I know if I feed it by spending time in Your Word, it will grow, if I don't, it will die. And that's how I know, that of all the people in my life, You love me most!

24

THERE'S HOPE FOR YOU!

"I have...plans to give you the future you hope for."

JEREMIAH 29:11 MSG

*I*n Jeremiah 29:11 we have a great promise in a not-so-great chapter. So, if things aren't going too well in your life right now, this verse is for you! God's people were living as slaves in Babylon. Why? Because of disobedience to God. And worse, Babylon was about as pagan as you could get. It wasn't the kind of place Christians hung out; it was a moral and spiritual wasteland. And on top of that, the Israelites' own preachers were leading them astray. So, God told them, "Don't let all those so-called preachers and know-it-alls...take you in with their lies" (Jeremiah 29:8-9 MSG). Yet in the midst of all this, along comes the God of hope saying, "I still have a plan for you. It's not over till I say so. I'm going to turn things around for you. Your best days are ahead." You say, "How do you know that God still has a plan for me?" Because you're still breathing! He has a plan for every single person He ever created, and it never goes out of date. Unlike the milk in your supermarket that has an expiration date on it after which it can't be used, God's plans don't have expiration dates. Even if you've missed His plan entirely for years, that plan can still swing into operation the moment you turn your life over to Him and fall in line with His will. Now, your plan might be somewhat modified from what it would have been 20 years ago if you'd paid attention, but that doesn't stop God. He can adapt to fit anything that comes up, in any life that's ever lived—including yours. So, there's hope for you!

PRAYER

Lord, it's humbling to think that I am so important to You, that you created a plan for my life before I was born. I've taken too many offramps during our journey together, but You have always been waiting at the end of the ramp, to get me back on track. You do this because You love me.

_____
_____
_____
_____

GOD'S PART

Lord, I know that I can't do Your part, and You won't do mine. So I trust you to:

_____
_____
_____
_____

MY PART

_____
_____
_____
_____

> I am important to You God, and You have a plan for my life. The best part is, You never give up on me when I miss the mark. And that's how I know, that of all the people in my life, You love me most!

25

WHERE IS GOD IN
THE STORM?

"When neither sun nor stars appeared for
many days and the storm continued raging, we
finally gave up all hope of being saved."

ACTS 27:20 NIV

There are times when God seems inaccessible. When you pray, you feel abandoned in your present circumstances. And not just abandoned, but terrified and even hopeless. Paul understood that feeling. He'd longed for an opportunity to preach in Rome and was on his way there when a hurricane destroyed his ship. Paul not only foresaw the loss of the ship, its crew and cargo, but "our own lives also" (Acts 27:10 NIV). He tried to warn the crew of the impending tragedy, but his words were disregarded by those in charge. In short, Paul and 276 others were placed in a life-threatening position by the willful disregard of others, and there was nothing he could do about it. Feeling a sense of despair, he and his believing companions declared, "We finally gave up all hope of being saved!" Then after fourteen days lost at sea—when the hurricane was fiercest—God sent an angel. "Do not be afraid, Paul...God has graciously given you the lives of all who sail with you" (Acts 27:24 NIV). When it looked like Paul's consuming desire to preach in Rome would be thwarted, God faithfully piloted them through the storm to the exact destination He'd planned for them. Are you caught in a storm? Whatever trial you're facing today, know this one thing: You can trust God to carry you through it.

PRAYER

Father, I didn't see this one coming. My first thoughts were that You had abandoned me, so my hope and faith melted on the ground. Please forgive me. I will remind myself of Who I'm serving, and that You always have a way of escape so I can trust You in this storm.

_____

_____

_____

_____

GOD'S PART

Lord, I know that I can't do Your part, and You won't do mine. So I trust you to:

_____

_____

_____

_____

MY PART

_____

_____

_____

_____

Lord, it's taking me some time to learn to trust in You through every battle. I don't always see what You're doing behind the scenes, but I know You're there. You never fail me. And that's how I know, that of all the people in my life, You love me most!

26

WHILE YOU'RE WAITING

"Multiply there and do not decrease."

JEREMIAH 29:6 NASB

*G*od tells His people "I know the plans I have for you...plans to prosper you...plans to give you hope and a future" (Jeremiah 29:11 NIV). But hope needs a nurturing environment. God didn't give them permission to take that hope, then just sit back and do nothing. No, He told them exactly what He wanted them to do while He was working out some of the details for their future: "Build houses and settle down; plant gardens and eat what they produce...Also, seek the peace and prosperity of the city to which I have carried you...Pray to the Lord for it, because if it prospers, you too will prosper" (Jeremiah 29:5-7 NIV). In other words, while you're waiting for God to turn things around, seize the moment. Become as productive as you possibly can. Maximize your potential. A lot of us, while we wait for God to work, think we can do nothing when there's plenty around to do. God said, "Pray for the prosperity of those around you, because when they prosper you will too." A lot of us don't understand this. We've become concerned about one person only—ourselves. When we mess up, the only person we tend to see is ourselves. But God says, "While you're waiting on me to do something good for you, begin doing something good for others." That's what Paul meant, "It is more blessed to give than to receive" (Acts 20:35 NASB). Then he added: "The Lord will reward each one for whatever good they do" (Ephesians 6:8 NIV). You see, by blessing others you literally open a channel for God to come through when He blesses you.

PRAYER
Lord, When I start putting my thoughts and energy into obeying those things You've directed me to do, as well as making myself available to help someone else, it takes the focus off of me and helps me to maintain my hope and faith while I wait for You to answer my prayer.

_____
_____
_____
_____

GOD'S PART
Lord, I know that I can't do Your part, and You won't do mine. So I trust you to:

_____
_____
_____
_____

MY PART

_____
_____
_____
_____

Father, while I am waiting for You to answer my prayer,
I will look for ways I can serve You and show Your love
to others who are hurting. And that's how I know,
that of all the people in my life, You love me most!

COURAGE

27

DON'T BE AFRAID, GOD IS WITH YOU

"I am your shield, your very great reward."

GENESIS 15:1 NIV

hen God sends you into a new situation or asks you to do something you've never done before, you'll experience uncertainty and fear, and have a lot of questions. God knows that; that's why the promise He gives you is always equal to the project He gives you. Imagine selling your house, packing up your belongings, putting your family in the car, and heading down the road without having a clue where you're going. Sound crazy? That's what God asked Abraham to do. But He told him, "Do not be afraid...I am your shield, your very great reward" (Genesis 15:1). The word "shield" means God will protect you, and the word "reward" means He will provide everything you need. Does that mean you won't experience fear? No, it means you must trust Him in spite of your fears! Dr. Bernard Vittone says: "As we age, we lose the ability to distinguish between the negative anxiety associated with work, stress, and tension, and the positive type that's a natural and exciting part of trying something new. As a result, we become more fearful and avoid anxiety-producing situations. When that happens, the desire for safety keeps us stuck in neutral. Trying to avoid risk is like trying to avoid living; without a goal to strive for you stop growing altogether." If Abraham had refused to obey God because he feared the unknown and the untried, he'd have missed his "very great reward." So, press through your fear today and claim the blessing God has promised you on the other side of it. Don't be afraid; God is with you!

PRAYER

Father, I'm not sure if I will ever get to the place where I am so full of faith that I won't experience fear, but I'm going to try. The more I learn about Your faithfulness, the more I see how pointless it is to fear at all. Thank you for staying so close to me and for helping me overcome my fears.

GOD'S PART

Lord, I know that I can't do Your part, and You won't do mine. So I trust you to:

MY PART

Lord, You are my shield and my provision in all things. You are constantly nudging me to grow in the Word and trust You more. And that's how I know, that of all the people in my life, You love me most!

28

COURAGE WITH COLD FEET

"Benaiah...went down into a pit on a
snowy day and killed a lion."

2 SAMUEL 23:20 NIV

Benaiah was one of King David's "mighty men." His résumé reads: "Benaiah...was a valiant fighter...He...went down into a pit on a snowy day and killed a lion." That's what is called "courage with cold feet." The greatest courage of all is showing courage in the face of fear. Someone said, "Courage is just fear that has said its prayers." When you know you have heard clearly from God, you are filled with faith in that moment. It puts steel in your spine. But then as you move out in faith, you encounter the lions of fear. "What if this doesn't work? What if I fail? What will people say?" Suddenly you're having an attack of the "what ifs." Mark Twain said, "Courage is resistance to fear, mastery of fear, not absence of fear." You must decide whether you're going to become a warrior—or a worrier. There's no middle ground. When you're faced with a health crisis or a family crisis or a financial crisis, you either choose to stand on God's Word and fight or give in to worry. This side of heaven we will never fully understand why bad things happen to good people. But we know that God is good—all the time! So, when bad things happen, you will either give in to fear and allow it to destroy your peace and well-being, or you will become a warrior armed with God's Word and rise up against it. When fear threatens to engulf your mind, stand up with the Psalmist and say, "Whenever I am afraid, I will trust in You" (Psalm 56:3 NKJV).

PRAYER

Lord, I never really think to call what I'm feeling fear, but You've helped me see that's exactly what it is. I've been afraid to stay and to go, to give and to take, to believe and not believe. Teach me to turn off the "what if" game in my head. Instead of thinking of all the things that can go wrong, help me to see all the things that can go right.

_____

_____

_____

_____

GOD'S PART

Lord, I know that I can't do Your part, and You won't do mine. So I trust you to:

_____

_____

_____

MY PART

_____

_____

_____

_____

Some days I have courage and feel I can conquer the world, and other days it slips through my fingers so easily. But You are always with me, encouraging me to stand and not give up. And that's how I know, that of all the people in my life, You love me most!

29

WHAT TO DO IN A CRISIS

"We gave way to it and were driven along."

ACTS 27:15 NIV

*D*on't drift. Typically, we react to a crisis in the same three ways as the sailors on board Paul's ship: "The ship was caught by the storm and could not head into the wind; so we gave way to it and were driven along." The first thing life's storms tend to do is make us drift. We lose sight of our goals and forget where we're headed. We ignore our values and get off course. Because they weren't equipped with compasses and the stars were obscured by the storm, the sailors were in total darkness. Which raises the question: How do you characteristically react in a dark situation when you can't see the stars and you don't have a compass? You drift. You go where the waves carry you. You let your problems batter you and toss you back and forth. In life, strong currents can discourage you and make you wonder, "What's the use? Why fight it?" So, you end up going with the flow. But now's the time to do the opposite! Strengthen your grip of faith: "Hold unswervingly to the hope we profess, for he who promised is faithful...Do not throw away your confidence; it will be richly rewarded...persevere so that when you have done the will of God, you will receive what he has promised" (Hebrews 10:23, 35-36 NIV). Note the phrase: "He who promised is faithful." Question: Has God ever failed you? Answer: No! And He won't now. "Hold unswervingly to the hope we profess...he who promised is faithful" (Hebrews 10:23 NIV), and He will bring you through this crisis.

80

PRAYER

Father, how many times have I asked the question, "How did I get into this mess?" And the simple answer is, I left You out of the process. As You help me to develop my faith more and more, help me to quickly notice when I get off track and give me the courage to step back onto the right path.

_____
_____
_____
_____

GOD'S PART

Lord, I know that I can't do Your part, and You won't do mine. So I trust you to:

_____
_____
_____
_____

MY PART

_____
_____
_____
_____

Staying calm in the middle of the storm is a gift I can give myself, but I can't do it without Your grace. When I choose to stay calm, I can hear Your still small voice saying, "This is the way walk in it." And that's how I know, that of all the people in my life, You love me most!

30

WHAT TO DO WHEN YOU DON'T KNOW WHAT TO DO

"Don't worry about anything; instead, pray about
everything. Tell God what you need and thank him for all
he has done. Then you will experience God's peace."

PHILIPPIANS 4:6 NLT

*N*ever rule out the possibility of a miracle. Worry is faith in the wrong thing. Our God is in the miracle business. Jesus said, "With God all things are possible" (Mark 10:27 KJV). Until you have talked with God, you have not heard the last word on the subject. Next, position yourself to receive. Blind Bartimaeus positioned himself where he knew Jesus would be passing by, and even though the disciples tried to keep him quiet, he cried that much louder, saying, "Jesus, thou son of David, have mercy on me" (Mark 10:47 KJV). What a miracle! The first face Bartimaeus saw was the face of Jesus. Go to God's house; get with God's people; get into God's Word. That is where you will find God. Next, raise the level of your faith. "Anyone who comes to [God] must believe" (Hebrews 11:6 NIV). Do the people in your life strengthen your faith or increase your fear? Do they lift you up or pull you down? The reason the early disciples saw such miracles was, "They worshipped together at the Temple each day, met in homes for the Lord's Supper, and shared their meals with great joy and generosity" (Acts 2:46 NLT). Some of us hardly make it to church once a week. We don't fellowship with each other over the things of God or take the time to praise Him or spend time in prayer, then we wonder why nothing seems to be working. Come on! It's time to expect a miracle, to position yourself to receive it and start building up your faith!

PRAYER

Lord, when I am worried and don't know what to do, help me feed on Your Word, fellowship with You in prayer, and surround myself with people who strengthen my faith, not increase my fear. If I do this, I know I will experience Your peace.

_____

_____

_____

_____

GOD'S PART

Lord, I know that I can't do Your part, and You won't do mine. So I trust you to:

_____

_____

_____

_____

MY PART

_____

_____

_____

_____

Father, when I find myself in the position of not having a clue what to do, I choose You. You are the solution to all my problems. And that's how I know, that of all the people in my life, You love me most!

31

YOU CAN OVERCOME
YOUR FEARS

"When I am afraid, I will put my trust in you."

PSALM 56:3 NLT

*I*s fear causing you to hide from somebody today? Your boss? Your husband or wife? Your strong-willed child? Your grouchy coworker? When God asked Adam, "'Where are you?' He replied...'I hid...I was afraid'" (Genesis 3:9-10 NLT). And we've all been hiding from things ever since. We hide behind forced smiles, agreeable words we don't mean, and social rituals we detest. Or worse, we hide behind things we do believe but don't express because we are afraid of what people might think or say. We try to avoid the pain of confronting someone, and the emotional energy we're afraid we'll have to invest in cleaning up afterwards. Short-term it may be easier to act as if things don't bother you or pretend to agree when in reality you disagree. But long-term it doesn't work, because peace isn't the absence of discord. When we remain silent in order to avoid confrontation, we just end up avoiding something far more important—relationships. For example, when we don't speak up on the job because we fear making waves, we end up resentful, alienated from our fellow workers, and maybe losing an opportunity to make things better. When we're afraid to confront our marriage partner (and this should be done in love, not anger), we end up emotionally distant. When we refuse to share our faith because we're afraid of being ridiculed, we lose the opportunity to bring hope to someone who really needs it. So, rise up and say, "When I am afraid, I will put my trust in You." Confront your fears, come out of hiding, and start living.

PRAYER

Father, so often I become fearful when I must make a major decision or confront something or someone in my life. Your Word tells me not to be afraid. Today I ask You to give me courage and help me put my trust in You so that I can overcome my fears.

_____

_____

_____

_____

GOD'S PART

Lord, I know that I can't do Your part, and You won't do mine. So I trust you to:

_____

_____

_____

_____

MY PART

_____

_____

_____

_____

I had no idea how much of my life has been ruled by fear. But I've noticed how You bring up one issue at a time, and You help me overcome it. And that's how I know, that of all the people in my life, You love me most!

PURPOSE

32

THE PERSON YOU
WERE MADE TO BE

"We are...created...to do good works,
which God prepared in advance."

EPHESIANS 2:10 NIV

*G*od created you, and He knows what you were intended to be. He has "good works" for you to do, but they're not necessarily the kind of "to do" things we put on a list for our spouses or employees. They're signposts to your true self. Your spiritual life isn't limited to certain devotional activities. It is about being empowered by God to become the person He envisioned when He created you. But just as nobody becomes happy because their goal is to be happy, becoming the person God intended you to be won't happen if your focus is always on yourself. Flourishing is tied to a nobler vision; it doesn't happen by "looking out for number one." People who flourish bring blessing to others, and they do it in unexpected and humble circumstances. Every once in a while, you catch a glimpse of the person you were made to be. You say something inspirational. You express compassion. You forgive an old hurt. You give sacrificially. You refrain from saying something you'd normally blurt out. And as you do, you glimpse for a moment the reason God made you. Only He knows your full potential, and He's always guiding you toward the best version of yourself. He uses many tools, He's never in a hurry—and that can be frustrating. But even in our frustration He's at work producing patience. He never gets discouraged by how long it takes, and He delights every time you grow. Only God can see the "best version of you," and He's more concerned with your reaching your full potential than you are.

PRAYER
Lord, I read in Your Word that You had a plan for me before I was even born. Guide me and help me become the person You intend me to be. I want to live the life You have planned for me so I can honor You and reach my full potential.

_____
_____
_____
_____

GOD'S PART
Lord, I know that I can't do Your part, and You won't do mine. So I trust you to:

_____
_____
_____
_____

MY PART

_____
_____
_____
_____

> I know that I don't have to do anything more than discover and follow Your plan for my life. And that's how I know, that of all the people in my life, You love me most!

33

GOD IS WORKING IT OUT FOR YOU

"God...calls things into being that were not."

ROMANS 4:17 NIV

*Y*ou must believe what God says about you, over what everyone else says! You might've had a bad childhood, or a failed marriage or career. "Forgetting those things which are behind, and reaching forward to those things which are ahead" (Philippians 3:13 NKJV). The Bible doesn't say that we call those things which are not as though they are. Nor does it say others have the power to speak things which are not as though they are over your life. No, it is God, through His Word, Who speaks into existence His will for your life. And you should be glad about that. You wouldn't want anybody else to have power to determine your destiny. Our responsibility is to line up our will with God's will. When we do, He empowers us to accomplish what normally would be humanly impossible. The Bible says, "The just shall live by faith" (Romans 1:17 NKJV). Your faith is more important than your performance. Yes, when God decrees something, we get to participate in it. But in every case, it's God who performs it. The thing you're worried about performing, God says will be done through His power. Will you experience delays and disappointments? Yes, but ultimately you won't be denied, for God has decreed it. You say, "But what about all my unanswered questions or all the loose ends that need to be tied up?" Listen: "All things work together for good to those who love God, to those who are the called according to His purpose" (Romans 8:28 NKJV). Relax; God is working it out for you.

PRAYER

Father, so often I listen to the opinions of those who say I will never amount to anything. Only You control my destiny. Help me to shut out every voice but Your voice, to walk by faith, and know that You are working everything out for my good.

_____

_____

_____

_____

GOD'S PART

Lord, I know that I can't do Your part, and You won't do mine. So I trust you to:

_____

_____

_____

_____

MY PART

_____

_____

_____

_____

I know that if I was able to see the future, I'd want to run and hide. I don't have to worry about what I can't see, because You are just out of sight working on my behalf. And that's how I know, that of all the people in my life, You love me most!

34

GOD'S CUSTOMIZED
PLAN FOR YOUR LIFE

"To will and to act in order to fulfill his good purpose."

PHILIPPIANS 2:13 NIV

*G*od is committed to His plan for your life, not yours! You can't say, "Lord, here's my plan; bless it." He may, but He may not. "He...created us...so we can do the good things he planned for us" (Ephesians 2:10 NLT). You can't say, "In this category I'm doing things my way, but in that category, I'm being led by God." No, every step you take must be synchronized by the beat of the Holy Spirit. Nothing should be more important to you than keeping pace with Him. Paul writes: "For it is God who works in you to will and to act according to his...purpose" (Philippians 2:13 NIV). God works through you as you open your spirit, engage your mind, and use your talents to do what He's already put into your heart. The moment you say yes, He gives you the power to perform His will. Notice, He doesn't reveal His will, then call you. No, He calls you, and as you step out and obey Him, He reveals His will to you step by step. Each day God is molding you into a greater likeness of His Son. That's His objective. You're not out for a stroll, you're going somewhere! Over and over again you'll be put into situations that mature you to the point where you have the same attitude, the same perspective, the same responses, and the same discernment as Jesus. Once you understand that, walking with God will take on a whole new meaning. You'll realize that His customized plan for your life is the only plan that will ever satisfy you.

PRAYER

Lord, I always want to know what comes next, but that's not how You work. My steps are ordered by You. As I obey, You will reveal Your plan for my life, and that's why I need to stay in constant contact with You through prayer.

_____

_____

_____

_____

GOD'S PART

Lord, I know that I can't do Your part, and You won't do mine. So I trust you to:

_____

_____

_____

_____

MY PART

_____

_____

_____

_____

God, You bring people across my path when I need them most, and You put me in front of others to be a blessing to them. And that's how I know, that of all the people in my life, You love me most!

35

DON'T DISCARD YOUR TOMORROWS!

"Tomorrow the Lord will do wonders among you."

JOSHUA 3:5 NASB

*Y*our yesterdays have made you what you are today, but your tomorrows can make you what God always intended you to become. Joshua was talking to a nation whose yesterdays were a long list of repeated failures and rebellion against God. They had been convicted, judged, punished, and reinstated frequently by the God they'd flagrantly sinned against. Surely, they ought to have been cut off from Him, stripped of any future blessing. But "Joshua said to the people, 'Consecrate yourselves, for tomorrow the Lord will do wonders among you.'" Consecrate yourself, realign yourself with God's plans and watch Him begin to work in your life. Just when the enemy has you convinced that with your past God couldn't possibly have a future for you, He calls you to prepare yourself so He can bless you. God is fully aware of your yesterdays, but He's much more focused on your tomorrows. Why do we discard our tomorrows when we so desperately need them? When Jesus cried, "It is finished!" (John 19:30 NKJV), His disciples concluded it was all over. So, they slipped away to contemplate the tomorrow they thought would never be. But with God, every ending is a new beginning, and three mornings later the angel announced the resurrection and the new tomorrow that would guarantee the future for all believers. "It (your yesterday) is finished!" Don't give up your tomorrows by building monuments to your past failures – "for tomorrow the Lord will do wonders among you."

PRAYER

Lord, I thank You that You are not focused on the failures of my past, You are much more focused on my future and making me into the person You intend me to be. Help me trust You with my tomorrow's.

_____
_____
_____
_____

GOD'S PART

Lord, I know that I can't do Your part, and You won't do mine. So I trust you to:

_____
_____
_____
_____

MY PART

_____
_____
_____
_____

> Sometimes I get so caught up in today, that I forget about tomorrow. I'm so grateful that Your still small voice is ever-present to guide me. And that's how I know, that of all the people in my life, You love me most!

36

HOW TO ACCOMPLISH GREAT THINGS

"Lord, let your ear be attentive to the
prayer of this your servant."

NEHEMIAH 1:11 NIV

*Y*ou must ask God for the plan. Why? Because the only plan He will bless is the one He gives you. Every good idea isn't necessarily a God-idea. The Bible says, "Many are the plans in a person's heart, but it is the Lord's purpose that prevails" (Proverbs 19:21 NIV). How will you know your plan lines up with God's plan, especially when you encounter obstacles and opposition? In two ways: (1) A fire will burn within you. Jeremiah said, "His word is in my heart like a fire...shut up in my bones. I am weary of holding it in; indeed, I cannot" (Jeremiah 20:9 NIV). When God places a burning desire within you, He will enable you to rise above the adverse circumstances that surround you. You'll find yourself drawn, driven, directed, and dedicated. You may not always be able to explain it to others, but you'll "know in your knower" that you are in the will of God. (2) God will show you the right path to take. "Along unfamiliar paths I will guide them; I will turn the darkness into light before them and make the rough places smooth. These are the things I will do; I will not forsake them" (Isaiah 42:16 NIV). Note the words "unfamiliar paths... darkness...rough places," but don't be thrown or discouraged by them. Instead, expect them! David said, "The Lord will work out his plans for my life—for your faithful love, O Lord, endures forever" (Psalm 138:8 NLT). And David's God is your God—He Hasn't changed one iota!

PRAYER

Lord, Your Word tells me that You wired us all differently and that You gave us different gifts and desires to draw us onto the path that You ordained for each of us. Speak to my heart. Help me to know the difference between a good idea and a God idea. I want to follow You.

_____

_____

_____

_____

GOD'S PART

Lord, I know that I can't do Your part, and You won't do mine. So I trust you to:

_____

_____

_____

_____

MY PART

_____

_____

_____

_____

I am unique. There is no one else like me in this world. You made me special. And that's how I know, that of all the people in my life, You love me most!

DIRECTION

37

DO YOU NEED DIRECTION?

_____

"The Lord watches over the path of the godly."

PSALM 1:6 NLT

*G*od will speak to you: (1) Through relationships. Sometimes He will give you direct revelation, but often He will speak to you through relationships. His Word says: "Remember your leaders, who spoke the word of God to you" (Hebrews 13:7 NIV). Who speaks into your life? To whom are you submitted? Without good input you will live unprotected and undirected. (2) Through your gifts. "A man's gift makes room for him" (Proverbs 18:16 NASB). When God is directing your steps, you won't need to kick the door open or force your way in. Your gift will bring a solution and meet a need; therefore, you'll be welcomed, valued, and rewarded. (3) Through your thoughts. "But we have the mind of Christ" (1 Corinthians 2:16 NIV). When our minds are renewed by His Word and lined up with His will, God actually thinks through us. Consider what an advantage that is! (4) Through open doors. Paul wrote, "Because a great door for effective work has opened to me, and there are many who oppose me" (1 Corinthians 16:9 NIV). God will open doors for you, but you must remember that with every opportunity He gives, challenges come too. That's what builds your faith and strengthens you for the future. (5) Through "a word" of confirmation. "Your ears will hear a voice behind you, saying, 'This is the way; walk in it'" (Isaiah 30:21 NIV). Note the word "behind." This word comes after you obey God, letting you know you've made a good decision and that you're on the right track. Yes, you can be led by God. His Word says: "The Lord watches over the path of the godly."

PRAYER

Father, I need direction in my life. I don't want to go down the wrong path. Line up my thoughts with Your thoughts and my ways with Your ways. Show me the path I need to take and help me to be led by Your Spirit.

_____
_____
_____
_____

GOD'S PART

Lord, I know that I can't do Your part, and You won't do mine. So I trust you to:

_____
_____
_____
_____

MY PART

_____
_____
_____
_____

When my mind is renewed by Your Word, You think Your thoughts through me. You guide me and lead me in the path I need to go. And that's how I know, that of all the people in my life, You love me most!

38

HOW TO PRAY WHEN YOU'RE WORRIED

"Don't worry about anything; instead, pray about
everything...Then you will experience God's peace...
His peace will guard your hearts and minds."

PHILIPPIANS 4:6-7 NLT

*A*re you worried today? Have you lost your peace of mind? Begin to pray this prayer until it takes root in your heart and becomes your fixed attitude: "Father, You told me not to be afraid because You are with me, You will uphold me, and those who come against me will not succeed (See Isaiah 41:10-11 KJV). You said no evil would come upon me, nor any plague touch my home for You have ordered Your angels to protect me (See Psalm 91:10-11 NKJV). You said when I walk through rivers of difficulty (when I'm 'in over my head') You won't let me drown, and when I walk through fires of adversity (when 'the heat is on') You won't allow me to get burned for You are watching over me (See Isaiah 43:2-3 NLT). You said no weapon formed against me shall prosper (See Isaiah 54:17 NKJV). I cannot keep the ene-my's weapons from being formed, but I know You will keep them from prospering. You said if I ask anything according to Your will, You would grant my request (See 1 John 5:14-15 NKJV). You said when I walk in obedience before You, I will be blessed when I come in and blessed when I go out, blessed when I lie down and blessed when I get up (See Deuteronomy 28:6 NKJV). You told me to give all my troubles to You and You would take care of me (See 1 Peter 5:7 NKJV). So here they are! Today I'm standing on Your Word. You said it! I believe it! That settles it! Amen."

PRAYER

Lord, when I find myself worrying and trying to fix things on my own, I will stop and pray. Your Word tells me if I pray, I will experience Your peace in my life. I need Your peace right now. Help me to not be afraid and place my trust in You.

_____
_____
_____
_____

GOD'S PART

Lord, I know that I can't do Your part, and You won't do mine. So I trust you to:

_____
_____
_____
_____

MY PART

_____
_____
_____
_____

> You are watching over me. You send Your angels
> to protect me. When I am in over my head, You
> rescue me. And that's how I know, that of all
> the people in my life, You love me most!

39

LESSONS LEARNED ON YOUR JOURNEY

"Call to me and I will...tell you...things you do not know."

JEREMIAH 33:3 NIV

*T*he secret of prayer. Do you feel lost in unfamiliar territory, uncertain as to what your next move should be? God uses such times to get your attention, call you back to Himself and encourage you to lean on Him, your unfailing source of strength and wisdom. Stop trying to figure everything out by yourself! God says, "Call to me and I will answer you and tell you...things you do not know." Take your problem to the Lord and ask Him for a solution; He won't disappoint you. "The prayer of a right-teous person is powerful and effective" (James 5:16 NIV). You learn the power of patience. When the Holy Spirit gives you direction and puts a goal or dream in your heart, it's easy to be quick on the trigger and want it to happen overnight. Timing is crucial. And it's under God's control, not yours! Waiting for God's timing isn't wasting time, it's essential in developing two quali-ties you need—faith and hope. "But if we hope for what we do not yet have, we wait for it patiently" (Romans 8:25 NIV). While you are learning patience, God is at work arranging things on your behalf, and producing Christlike qualities in you. The Psalmist said that his hope was in God. What's your hope in? Good luck? The economy? The doctor's prognosis? As long as your hope is in anything other than God's unfailing love and goodness, you'll wrestle with uncertainty. What's the answer? "Their hearts are steadfast, trusting in the Lord" (Psalm 112:7 NIV).

PRAYER

Lord, I understand that sometimes You are silent for a reason. Help me to remain steadfast as I await further instructions from You. And help me to not get ahead of You, because whatever You have planned is far better than anything I can imagine.

_____

_____

_____

_____

GOD'S PART

Lord, I know that I can't do Your part, and You won't do mine. So I trust you to:

_____

_____

_____

_____

MY PART

_____

_____

_____

_____

You understand that I am human, and that I don't always get it right. You know that I sometimes jump ahead of You, yet You lovingly guide me back to Your path. And that's how I know, that of all the people in my life, You love me most!

40

TAKE CONTROL
OF YOUR LIFE

"I have set before you life and death...choose life."

DEUTERONOMY 30:19 NKJV

*C*hoice is the greatest power God gave you. Too many of us just accept our lives—we don't become leaders of ourselves. As a result, we can't get out of our own way. Holocaust survivor Elie Wiesel wrote in *Souls on Fire* that when you die and go to meet your Maker, you're not going to be asked why you didn't become a Messiah or find a cure for cancer. All you're going to be asked is, "Why didn't you become you? Why didn't you become all that you are?" Fulfilling God's will for your life requires taking responsibility for yourself and your life. How do you do that? By saying yes to God first—then to yourself. Every time you say yes, you open yourself up to your God-given potential and to the greatest of possibilities. If you're used to saying no, you may find this difficult. If that is true in your case, then at least be willing to say "maybe." One day a father whose child was chronically ill asked Jesus to heal him. "Jesus said to him, 'If you can believe, all things are possible to him who believes.' Immediately the father of the child cried out and said with tears, 'Lord, I believe; help my unbelief!'" (Mark 9:23-24 NKJV). If you're a self-doubter, pray that same prayer. God will answer it. Never forget that you are unique, possessing talents, experiences, and opportunities that no one else has ever had—or ever will have. You're respon-sible to become all God made you to be, not only for your own benefit but for everyone else's.

PRAYER
Father, I want to live up to my God-given potential and become ALL that You intend me to be. I understand now that I don't need to compare myself with others, I just need to be the best version of me that I can be.

_____

_____

_____

_____

GOD'S PART
Lord, I know that I can't do Your part, and You won't do mine. So I trust you to:

_____

_____

_____

_____

MY PART

_____

_____

_____

_____

> Everything I need You have arranged for me to have
> at the very moment I need it. And that's how I know,
> that of all the people in my life, You love me most!

PROTECTION

41

DO YOU FEEL THREATENED?

"After they had prayed, the place where they were meeting was shaken. And they were all filled with the Holy Spirit."

ACTS 4:31 NIV

*D*o you feel like you're under attack today? If so, notice four things the Apostles did when they were threatened by the authorities for doing what God told them to do: (1) They brought God into the picture. "Lord, look on their threats" (Acts 4:29 NKJV). Have you talked to the Lord about it yet? If it's not big enough to be a prayer, it's too small to be a burden! God should be the first person you discuss it with, not the last. Prayer is the door through which He enters your situation, but you have to invite Him in. (2) They prayed for greater faith. "Lord...grant unto thy servants...boldness" (Acts 4:29 NKJV). It's unrealistic to expect that all your questions will be answered, and all your fears will disappear. Fear and faith will always be at work in your life. If you want to be an over-comer, learn to starve your fear and feed your faith (See Romans 10:17 NKJV). (3) They expected God to intervene. "Stretch out your hand" (Acts 4:30 NIV). The disciples had been through a terrible storm with Jesus so they knew what He could do: "About three o'clock in the morning Jesus came to them, walking on the water" (Matthew 14:25 NLT). And He still works the nightshift. He's available 24/7; all you need to do is call on Him! (4) They were all filled with the Holy Spirit (Acts 4:31 NLT). There's the key; they stayed energized and directed by the Spirit of God. And you must too. It's okay to use your gifts, as long as you lean only on God!

PRAYER

Lord, sometimes I wish that so much of the decision-making wasn't up to me. And then other times, I wish that I could make all the decisions about my life. But I know that I can't see the whole picture like You can. The only right choice I can make is to choose to include You in every aspect of my life.

_____
_____
_____
_____

GOD'S PART

Lord, I know that I can't do Your part, and You won't do mine. So I trust you to:

_____
_____
_____
_____

MY PART

_____
_____
_____
_____

> You say that I should not fear. You're covering me on all sides. You never slumber nor sleep. And that's how I know, that of all the people in my life, You love me most!

42

STANDING WHEN EVERYTHING AROUND YOU IS FALLING

"Let him who thinks he stands take heed lest he fall."

1 CORINTHIANS 10:12 NKJV

*T*he truth is: (1) Standing isn't inevitable, but it is possible! The moment you commit your life to Jesus, you're at war with Satan. And standing up to him requires staying armed. "Put on the full armor of God, so that you will be able to stand firm against the schemes of the devil" (Ephesians 6:11, 13 NASB). War is a casualty-laden business; you must take it as seriously as the enemy does, for the Bible says he's out "seeking someone to devour" (1 Peter 5:8 NASB). Be alert, but not alarmed. "A thousand may fall at your side…but it shall not [happen to] you" (Psalm 91:7 NASB). In conflict, some stand and some fall. The difference is, those who stand "have made the Lord…[their] dwelling place," whereas those who fall "make flesh [their] strength" (Jeremiah 17:5 NASB). (2) Falling isn't always preventable, but it's surmountable! It's not only the weak and immature who fall. Satan's strategy includes taking out the righteous, the unrighteous, the most vulnerable, and the least vulnerable. "A righteous man falls seven times, and rises again" (Proverbs 24:16 NASB). Now if the righteous fall so frequently, what's to be anticipated from everyone else? In war no one is guaranteed immunity from attack. But, "A good man… Though he fall, he shall not be utterly cast down: for the Lord upholds him with his hand" (Psalm 37:23-24 NKJV). Don't focus on the unable, or the disabled—but on Christ the Enabler!

PRAYER

Father, I am so good at thinking that I have everything under control. Even when I give everything over to You each morning, by the time I pour my second cup of coffee, I've pulled it right back. I don't want to live like this anymore. Please help me learn to stand perfectly still on Your Word in the eye of the storm.

_____

_____

_____

_____

GOD'S PART

Lord, I know that I can't do Your part, and You won't do mine. So I trust you to:

_____

_____

_____

_____

MY PART

_____

_____

_____

_____

When I hand my burdens over to You a hundred times, I will be sure I only take them back ninety-nine. Your patience with me is relentless. And that's how I know, that of all the people in my life, You love me most!

43

GOD IS LOOKING OUT FOR YOU!

"I will protect those who trust in my name."

PSALM 91:14 NLT

On a chilly March afternoon before going home for dinner, Pastor Walter Klempel fired up the church furnace in preparation for choir practice. When it was time to return to church with his family they were delayed because his daughter changed clothes. At the same time student Ladonna Vadergrift was struggling with a geometry problem and stayed home to work on it. Sisters Royena and Sadie Estes' car wouldn't start. Herbert Kipf lingered over a letter he'd put off writing. Joyce Black was feeling "plain lazy" and stayed home until the last minute. Pianist Marilyn Paul fell asleep after dinner and her mom, the choir director, had trouble waking her. Every single choir member was late; something that's never happened before nor since. Was it just a fluke? No! At 7:30 that night the West Side Church was flattened by an explosion from a gas leak, ignited by the furnace… directly below the empty choir loft! God said, "Before [you] call, I will answer" (Isaiah 65:24). God's looking out for you when you don't even know you're in danger! As His child you "live within the shadow of the Almighty, sheltered by…God…he rescues you from every trap, and protects you…His faithful promises are your armor…he orders his angels to protect you wherever you go" (Psalm 91:1-11 TLB). The Bible says: "The Angel of the Lord guards and rescues all who reverence him" (Psalm 34:7 TLB). You can call it coincidence, chance, fate, or you can call it what it really is – divine protection!

PRAYER

Lord, I don't know what is ahead in my life, but You do. I don't know where there are hidden dangers and potholes, but You do. Order my steps, direct my path, and keep me safe and secure in Your arms today.

_____

_____

_____

_____

GOD'S PART

Lord, I know that I can't do Your part, and You won't do mine. So I trust you to:

_____

_____

_____

_____

MY PART

_____

_____

_____

_____

I don't want to debate Your Word. I want to live in the fullness of Your Word. You say that I can pray and trust You to protect me. And that's how I know, that of all the people in my life, You love me most!

44

IN THE EYE OF THE STORM

"He who dwells in the secret place of the Most High
shall abide under the shadow of the Almighty."

PSALM 91:1 NKJV

The eye of the storm is the most peaceful place on earth. While wind and rain wreak havoc all around, pilots who fly storm-tracker planes say that all is perfectly still in that special place. In Psalm 91, David speaks about...terror...plagues...ten thousand falling at your right hand "but it will not come near you." Why? Listen: "He that dwelleth in the secret place of the Most High shall abide under the shadow of the Almighty. I will say of the Lord, He is my refuge and my fortress: my God; in Him will I trust. Surely He shall deliver [me]" (Psalm 91:1-3 NKJV). There are two ways to go through a storm: in panic or in peace. When a storm suddenly threatened their boat the disciples cried, "Do you not care that we are perishing?" (Mark 4:38 NKJV). And where was Jesus? Sleeping peacefully in the back of the boat. That's because He understood: (a) to get to where God wants to take you, you must go through certain storms. It's not optional; (b) when you're in the center of God's will the storm can't take you under; it's in the storm, not the calm, that you discover this; (c) when it's over you come out knowing God better, and more equipped to help others! "So trust in the Lord (commit yourself to Him, lean on Him, hope confidently in Him) forever; for the Lord God is an everlasting Rock [the rock of ages]" (Isaiah 26:4 AMPC). That's what it means to live in the eye of the storm!

PRAYER

Father, when I panic—over anything—it means that You are not my first thought. And if You're not my first thought when things go wrong, I'm in trouble. Please help me to be so full of Your Word, that no matter what goes on around me, I'm unphased and know exactly which Scriptures to stand on.

_____
_____
_____
_____

GOD'S PART

Lord, I know that I can't do Your part, and You won't do mine. So I trust you to:

_____
_____
_____
_____

MY PART

_____
_____
_____
_____

Jesus, Your disciples got scared while traveling by boat during a storm. And just like You were with them then, You are with me now. And that's how I know, that of all the people in my life, You love me most!

45

WHEN MICE ROAR

"His huge outstretched arms protect you
under them you're perfectly safe."

PSALM 91:4 MSG

*M*ax Lucado tells the following story. "Two-year-old Sarah sits on my lap. We're watching a comedy on television about a guy who has a mouse in his room. He is asleep. He opens one eye and finds himself peering into the face of the mouse. I laugh, but Sarah panics. She turns away from the screen and buries her face in my shoulder. Her little body grows rigid. She thinks the mouse is going to get her. "It's ok, Sarah," I assure her. Still, she's afraid. But with time I convince her, and she goes from white-knuckled fear, to peaceful chuckles. Why? Because her father spoke, and she believed him. Would to God that we could do the same! Got any giant mice on your screen? Got any fears that won't go away. I wish the fears were just television images. But they aren't. They lurk in hospital rooms and funeral homes. They stare at us from divorce papers and eviction notices. They glare through the eyes of a cruel parent, or an abusive mate. There are times when mice roar. Times when you need the strong arms of God to run to and hide in." Listen, "His huge outstretched arms protect you—under them you're perfectly safe...because God's your refuge...evil can't get close to you, harm can't get through the door. He orders His angels to guard you wherever you go. If you stumble, they'll catch you; their job is to keep you from falling" (Psalm 91:4-12 MSG). Today you have nothing to fear!

PRAYER

Lord, as I've been learning to pray the way You teach us to in Your Word, I can tell that I'm becoming more confident in You. I'm not where I want to be yet, but I am learning to let Your voice be the loudest voice I hear, no matter what is going on around me.

_____

_____

_____

_____

GOD'S PART

Lord, I know that I can't do Your part, and You won't do mine. So I trust you to:

_____

_____

_____

_____

MY PART

_____

_____

_____

_____

> If I were to panic this very moment, I know that I wouldn't stay that way for long. Your Word is taking root in me and teaching me to look to You for everything. And that's how I know, that of all the people in my life, You love me most!

46

GOD WILL BRING
YOU THROUGH

"The Father of compassion and the God of all comfort."

2 CORINTHIANS 1:3 NIV

*G*od can bring you through situations you think you won't survive, or feel you'll be stuck in forever. He can make you comfortable in the most uncomfortable places and give you peace in the midst of trauma. Before your life is over, you'll live, love, and experience loss. Losing some things will actually help you to appreciate the things you still have. It's the taste of failure that makes success sweet. You'll live each day not knowing what tomorrow holds, but confident that God has your tomorrows all planned out. They're not in the hands of your boss or your banker or your mate or anybody else. Nor are they in your own hands to manipulate and control. No, all your tomorrows are in God's hands. Just because you don't recognize the path you're on doesn't mean that God's not leading you. He promises, "I will lead them in paths they have not known. I will make darkness light before them, and crooked places straight. These things I will do for them, and not forsake them" (Isaiah 42:16 NKJV). So, get to know God—you'll need Him. And He'll be there for you. He'll be there when everybody and everything else has failed you. He'll be there for you in the dark places. "Weeping may endure for a night, but joy comes in the morning" (Psalm 30:5 NKJV). However long the night, morning always comes, and with it His joy. As you look back, you'll realize that His grace protected you, provided for you, secured you, calmed you, comforted you, and brought you through. Times and seasons change, but not God. He's always "the God of all comfort."

PRAYER
Father, I've noticed that You are very purposeful in every Word You use. And that helped me to recognize that You said that you would bring me through whatever I'm facing. You are trying to open my eyes to see that You want to help me get all the way through it to the other side. Thank you for being my answer and my solution to every trial.

_____
_____
_____
_____

GOD'S PART
Lord, I know that I can't do Your part, and You won't do mine. So I trust you to:

_____
_____
_____
_____

MY PART

_____
_____
_____
_____

There are so many things that I face in my life, but I can't allow myself to get stuck in the middle of it. Your Word says that You will bring me out of those tough seasons. And that's how I know, that of all the people in my life, You love me most!

47

HELP WHEN YOU NEED IT MOST!

"He leads me beside the still waters."

PSALM 23:2 NKJV

He leads me. God isn't behind you shouting, "Go!" He's in front of you clearing the path and showing you the way. At the curve He says, "Turn here." At the rise He whispers, "Step up." At the pothole He warns, "Watch your foot." He tells us what we need to know, when we need to know it. Listen: "We will find grace to help us when we need it most" (Hebrews 4:16 NLT). Note the word, "When." You say, "I don't know what I'll do if my husband dies." You will—when the time comes. "I don't know how I'll ever pay these bills." Jehovah Jireh, the Lord who provides will be there for you—when the time comes. "I'm not qualified to handle this, there's just too much I don't know." Maybe you want to know everything too soon. God will give you wisdom—when the time comes. The key is: meet today's problems with today's strength and leave tomorrow's in God's capable hands! During World War II, Arthur Sulzberger, publisher of the New York Times found it hard to sleep or rid his mind of fear, until he adopted these words from the hymn Lead Kindly Light: "I do not ask to see the distant scene; one step enough for me." God isn't going to let you see the distant scene either. He promises a lamp for your feet, not a crystal ball for your future. "He leads me" and that's enough for today! And tomorrow? "We will find grace to help us when we need it most" (Hebrews 4:16 NLT).

PRAYER

Lord, I always think I want to know everything that is in my future. But when I look back, I am grateful that I didn't because I would have worried myself sick over what was coming. You want my eyes on the present. Everything I need, You've already provided, no matter what I think or what I see. Please help me to learn to walk in that kind of faith.

_____

_____

_____

_____

GOD'S PART

Lord, I know that I can't do Your part, and You won't do mine. So I trust you to:

_____

_____

_____

_____

MY PART

_____

_____

_____

_____

I spend too much time thinking about the future, but not enough time thinking about today. You are teaching me how to be present in the moment. And that's how I know, that of all the people in my life, You love me most!

48

THIS YEAR LET GOD BE GOD IN YOUR LIFE

"Casting down imaginations..."

2 CORINTHIANS 10:5 KJV

How does God provide for us? One day at a time. Do you remember the Israelites in the wilderness? God fed them faithfully each day by sending manna from heaven. But some of them wanted to make sure they'd have enough for tomorrow, revealing their lack of trust in God, so they gathered more. But God would only allow them to collect enough for each day; when they tried to collect more the excess rotted. Understand this: When you worry over the future or things you can do nothing about, it's like trying to store up manna for tomorrow. Before you know it, you feel rotten. God wants you to give tomorrow's concerns to Him because they're too big for you. You only receive enough grace for today, so stay in the moment. Question: Are you being tormented by the "what ifs"? What if I get hurt or become ill, or the company downsizes, and I lose my job? What if people don't like or accept me? What if I can't find someone to love me and I end up alone? What if I'm not hearing from God and I make a mistake? The Bible calls this "imaginations"—you're imagining the worst-case scenario. Paul says, "Cast it down," for if you don't, you'll live in dread concerning things that haven't happened—and probably never will. What if you "figure it all out," then God surprises you and does something different, something better? All that time would be wasted. Haven't you already wasted enough time worrying? Here's an idea: This year relax and let God be God in your life!

PRAYER

I really don't know why I don't trust you more than I do, Lord. I tell my friends I'll pray for them, and when I do, I have faith that You will answer my prayer for them. But when I'm on the hot seat, all I see is failure. Forgive me and help me to always look at my circumstances through the filter of Your Word.

_____
_____
_____
_____

GOD'S PART

Lord, I know that I can't do Your part, and You won't do mine. So I trust you to:

_____
_____
_____
_____

MY PART

_____
_____
_____
_____

> You think big; I think small. You envision my success; I envision my failure. You are teaching me to change my perspective. And that's how I know, that of all the people in my life, You love me most!

49

WHAT YOU NEED IN THE WILDERNESS

"He led them on safely, so that they did not fear."

PSALM 78:53 NKJV

*Y*ou can be in the wilderness and still be in the center of God's will. "He made His own people go forth like sheep, and guided them in the wilderness like a flock…He led them on safely, so…they did not fear" (Psalm 78:52-53 NKJV). In the wilderness you get to know God in a way you never knew Him before. So, what else did Israel need to survive in the wilderness? Food! Someone calculated it would have taken about twenty-six train carloads of food to feed that many Israelites every day. The problem is there were no trains and no tracks! But they had something much better—God! For forty years He delivered manna, "the perfect food," to the doors of their tents. The supply was according to each family's individual need—and God never missed a day. So, if the economy has you feeling anxious and wondering whether or not God can take care of you—this is the word for you today! God may not give you everything you want, but He will give you everything you need. The God we serve doesn't suffer from lack or limitation! The Psalmist said, "I have been young, and now am old; yet I have not seen the righteous forsaken, nor his descendants begging bread" (Psalm 37:25 NKJV). The old country preacher got it right when he said, "Where He leads me, I will follow; what He feeds me I will swallow." Think of it: for forty years Israel never missed a meal or went without. And their God is your God, so put your trust in Him today and stop worrying!

PRAYER

Father, no matter what my need, I will look to You to meet it. Whatever I want, I will look to You to see if it's something You want me to have, or if You have a different plan. Shape my hopes and my desires to align with Your plan for my life. And no matter my circumstance, I will trust You and praise Your name.

_____

_____

_____

_____

GOD'S PART

Lord, I know that I can't do Your part, and You won't do mine. So I trust you to:

_____

_____

_____

_____

MY PART

_____

_____

_____

_____

I look at my surroundings and sometimes everything looks foreign to me. Other times, everything is familiar. But no matter where I am, You have promised to give me everything I need. And that's how I know, that of all the people in my life, You love me most!

50

ARE YOU STRUGGLING FINANCIALLY?

"All these things shall be added unto you."

MATTHEW 6:33 NKJV

*P*ray: "Heavenly Father, Your Word says, 'Seek ye first the kingdom of God, and his righteousness; and all these things shall be added unto you.' You are well able to take care of my financial situation. You know what needs to be done. Direct my steps (See Proverbs 3:5-6 KJV). Help me to remember that Your resources are meant to flow freely from the place of abundance to the place of need (See 2 Corinthians 8:14 KJV). I believe You have a financial plan for my life, and when fear of the future threatens to overwhelm me, I will hope continually and praise You more and more (See Psalm 71:14 KJV). As You walk with me through this crisis and I stay focused on You, You promised to keep me in perfect peace (See Isa 26:3 KJV). Forgive me for worrying. I cast all my cares on You right now (See 1 Peter 5:7 KJV). I don't have to bear these burdens on my own. I lay them down and receive Your divine rest (See Matthew 11:28 KJV). You promised to supply all my needs (See Philippians 4:19 KJV); that it's Your good pleasure to give me the [blessings and ben-efits of Your] kingdom (See Luke 12:32 KJV). You told me not to worry about anything and instead make my requests known to You with thanksgiving (See Philippians 4:6-7 KJV). I know You'll take care of tomorrow because You're Jehovah Jireh, my pro-vider (See Matthew 6:34 NKJV). You know what I need and when I need it...You're the God of more than enough (See Ephesians 3:20 NKJV). Thank You for meeting my every need. Amen."

PRAYER
Pray the prayer on the previous page.

_____

_____

_____

_____

GOD'S PART
Lord, I know that I can't do Your part, and You won't do mine.
So I trust you to:

_____

_____

_____

_____

MY PART

_____

_____

_____

_____

Lord, every time I look to Your Word, I find yet another
promise You've made to take care of me. You've not
left out a single thing. And that's how I know, that
of all the people in my life, You love me most!

51

EXPECT GOOD THINGS FROM GOD

"The eyes of all look expectantly to You."

PSALM 145:15 NKJV

When God introduced Himself to Abraham, He went by the name El Shaddai, which means "The provider of all." And today God is saying to you, "I will be all you need!" Now you know that God is able, but don't you sometimes wonder if He's willing? Simply having a revelation of God's ability is not enough; you must also believe that He will, in order to put a solid foundation under your faith. One day a leper came to Jesus saying, "If you are willing you can make me clean." Jesus revealed His heart by saying, "I am willing" (See Mark 1:40-42 NKJV). Don't allow Satan to convince you that God may or may not take care of you. The Bible says, "God shall supply all your need" (Philippians 4:19 NKJV). Notice, the Bible doesn't say, "God is power," it says, "God is love." It focuses on His willingness to use His power, rather than the power itself. Because God has a heart of love, He will use His power to meet your needs. God gets great pleasure out of meeting your needs. "The Lord is gracious and full of compassion, slow to anger and great in mercy. The Lord is good to all, and His tender mercies are over all His works... The eyes of all look expectantly to You, and You give them their food in due season. You open Your hand and satisfy the desire of every living thing" (Psalm 145:8-9 & 15-16 NKJV). God may not answer your prayer in the way you think He should, or when you think He should, but if you trust Him, He will answer in the way that's best for you.

PRAYER

Father, I thank You that You are the provider of all good things and that You want to answer my prayers. Sometimes I am fearful and doubt, but I am reminded in Your Word that I am to have faith and trust You to answer in the way You see best for me. Today I will stand in faith expecting good things from You.

_____

_____

_____

_____

GOD'S PART

Lord, I know that I can't do Your part, and You won't do mine. So I trust you to:

_____

_____

_____

_____

MY PART

_____

_____

_____

_____

Even when I doubt You still love me. I am grateful that You never give up on me and that You are always planning good things for my life. And that's how I know, of all the people in my life, You love me most!

52

GOD IS YOUR
UNFAILING SOURCE

"The brook dried up."

1 KINGS 17:7 NIV

*T*he Psalmist wrote, "Joyful are those...whose hope is in the Lord their God" (Psalm 146:5 NLT). One author writes: "Sometimes when there's not enough money to make ends meet, people tell us to budget, and we chuckle. We look at the situation and say, 'No way.' That's the time to trust God. Your possibilities aren't limited by past or present circumstances. If there's not enough to pay legitimate expenses, do your best and then let go. Trust God to supply your need, then look beyond your wallet. Look to your source. Claim a divine, unlimited supply. Do your part. Strive for financial responsibility in thought and action. Ask for wisdom and listen to God's leadings. Then let go of your fears and your need to control. We all know money is a necessary part of living— and so does God." F. B. Meyer said: "The education of our faith is incomplete till we learn that God's providence works through loss...There's a ministry to us through the failure and fading of things. The dwindling brook where Elijah sat is a picture of our lives! 'Some time later the brook dried up' (1 Kings 17:7 NIV) is the history of our yesterdays and the prophecy of our tomorrows. We must learn the difference between trusting in the gift and trusting in the Giver. The gift may last for a season, but the Giver is eternal. If the Lord had led Elijah directly to the widow at Zarephath, he'd have missed something that helped make him a better man— living by faith. Whenever our earthly resources dry up, it's so we may learn that our hope and health are in God."

PRAYER

Lord, when my needs are met, I can sometimes forget to come back and thank You. And when I have a need that I can't meet by myself, I come running to You for help. I know it's a good thing to look to You. So, I will praise You when I have much, and when I have little. And I will stop taking credit for what I have because without You, I would have absolutely nothing.

_____

_____

_____

_____

GOD'S PART

Lord, I know that I can't do Your part, and You won't do mine. So I trust you to:

_____

_____

_____

_____

MY PART

_____

_____

_____

_____

Even when the brook dries up You are still my source. When I have nothing left but God, I have enough to begin again. And that's how I know, of all the people in my life, You love me most!

HEALING

53

BELIEVE GOD FOR
YOUR HEALING

"I am the Lord, who heals you."

EXODUS 15:26 NIV

*I*n the Bible one of the names God chooses to be called by is "Jehovah Rapha," which means "I am the Lord who heals." Now, if God calls Himself the healer, then you have the right to believe what He says and expect that, given an opportunity, He will perform His role competently. After all, His credibility depends on living up to His name. The Psalmist said, "Your promises are backed by all the honor of your name" (Psalm 138:2 NLT). Has God changed? No; He says, "I am the Lord All-Powerful, and I never change" (Malachi 3:6 CEV). And Jesus, who is God, is "the same yesterday and today and forever" (Hebrews 13:8 NIV). What He was, He still is. What He did, He still does. So, when you or a loved one is sick, do these two things: (1) Pray, in faith believing. A "good faith" deal requires that both parties trust each other's word. Their trust is a rational decision of their will, not their emotions. Faith is your will deciding that God will keep the promise He has made to you. It's refusing to be ambivalent by saying, "If only I felt more positive." No business could survive such ambiguity. Jesus spelled it out clearly: "All things for which you pray and ask, believe that you have received them, and they will be granted you" (Mark 11:24 NASB). (2) Look for faith-partners who will pray with you. "Pray for each other so that you may be healed" (James 5:16 NLT). "If two of you agree...concerning anything you ask, my Father in heaven will do it for you" (Matthew 18:19 NLT).

PRAYER

Father, some days I feel so full of faith that I think I could pray and believe You to heal everyone in my neighborhood. Other days, I can't muster up enough faith to cure a headache. But it's me that changes, not You. Not Your Word. Please help me to have unwavering faith.

_____

_____

_____

_____

GOD'S PART

Lord, I know that I can't do Your part, and You won't do mine. So I trust you to:

_____

_____

_____

_____

MY PART

_____

_____

_____

_____

> Your Word declares You are my healer. Your promises stand forever, and You never change. You are teaching me to look only to You! And that's how I know, that of all the people in my life, You love me most!

54

STANDING ON HIS PROMISE

"He who comes to God must believe that...He is a rewarder."

HEBREWS 11:6 NASB

*L*ittle Christopher Pylant's parents refused to believe there was no hope for their son, who'd been diagnosed with a malignant brain tumor. After studying the x-rays, neurosurgeon Ben Carson told them, "There's no way I can encourage you." "The experts told us that in Georgia," the mother replied, "But God led us to Baltimore and said there's a doctor here who can help him. We believe you're that doctor." Carson replied, "I'll do my best," praying for a miracle. When he operated, Christopher's brain stem looked like it had been consumed by cancer, and without that there's no real life. In the waiting room he told the Pylants, "I'm sorry I couldn't help your son. We've all prayed but sometimes God works in ways we don't understand." They never wavered, saying, "God's going to heal our son. We're standing on His promise." Carson admired their faith, but the evidence was irrefutable. For three days little Christopher was comatose, but his eyes were focusing, and his physical movements improved. Following another scan Carson re-operated, and after removing the cancerous mass in layers and cleaning out the crevices, there it was—a healthy brain stem, distorted, but intact! Taking their son home a month later, his parents and the doctor thanked God together for a miracle. "He who comes to God must believe that...He is a rewarder of those who seek Him." The neurosurgeon said, "As they walked out of the hospital that day...glory shone on their faces, and I heard my mother telling me again, 'If you ask God for something believing He'll do it...He'll do it.'"

PRAYER

Lord, there are changes I need to make so I can stand on Your promises like You want me to. I commit to having what You say on any matter be the only outcome I envision, talk about, and praise You for. Even when what I see, feel, or hear are contrary to Your Word, I will choose to believe You. Help me to believe You—every time.

_____

_____

_____

_____

GOD'S PART

Lord, I know that I can't do Your part, and You won't do mine. So I trust you to:

_____

_____

_____

MY PART

_____

_____

_____

_____

Father, the Bible is full of promises You've made
to cover everything that could possibly arise
in my life. And that's how I know, that of all
the people in my life, You love me most!

55

HOW TO BE MADE WHOLE

"Jesus answered and said, 'Were there not ten
cleansed? But where are the nine?'"

LUKE 17:17 NKJV

*L*et's read how Jesus healed these ten lepers and see what
we can learn: (1) They seized the moment. "They lifted up
their voices and said, 'Jesus, Master, have mercy on us!'" (Luke
17:13 NKJV). Desperate people pray desperate prayers. Who
cares about propriety and outward appearances when you're
dying? These men realized that Jesus was "passing through"
(See Luke 17:11), and the worst thing that could happen was for
Him to pass them by. So, they seized the moment and cried out
to Him. And you can do that too, because nobody can hear you
like God (See Psalm 118:5 NKJV). (2) They had to walk it out.
Their healing wasn't immediate; it was a step-by-step process.
"And so it was that as they went, they were cleansed" (Luke 17:14
NKJV). Often that's the way it works. And it's not just one step,
but a commitment to plow through the obstacles and fears until
you get to your miracle. But it's worth the effort, and you appreciate your deliverance more when you have to walk it out day
by day depending on God. (3) Only one out of the ten returned
to give thanks. That's why Jesus asked, "Where are the nine?"
Were they too busy? Or too self-absorbed? Or just forgetful?
Notice what Jesus said to the one who came back: "Your faith
has made you well" (Luke 17:19 NKJV). Physical healing is often
accomplished through medicine, but you become "whole" in
body, mind, and soul by spending time worshiping the Lord and
getting to know Him.

PRAYER

Father, I don't have to understand how You are going to heal me. My job is to believe You'll do what You promised. So, I will take each step that You lay out before me, and I will trust You one step at a time, until I am whole. And I will thank You and praise You all along the journey.

_____

_____

_____

_____

GOD'S PART

Lord, I know that I can't do Your part, and You won't do mine. So I trust you to:

_____

_____

_____

_____

143

MY PART

_____

_____

_____

_____

> You want me to be whole and complete in You. Whether it's an unexpected diagnosis, an addiction, or something I've done to myself. And that's how I know, that of all the people in my life, You love me most!

56

YOU HAVE THE
POWER—USE IT!

"I pray that...he may strengthen you with power
through his Spirit in your inner being."

EPHESIANS 3:16 NIV

*U*ntil you realize the power of God that's within you, you won't use it. One of the greatest healing forces in the world is God's Word, and it's at your fingertips! For example, when you or a loved one gets sick, the Bible says, "These signs will follow those who believe: In My name they will...lay hands on the sick, and they will recover" (Mark 16:17-18 NKJV). That's a power-filled promise. When Jesus returned to Capernaum, the Bible says, "It was heard that He was in the house" (Mark 2:1 NKJV). And before He left there, a paralyzed man got up and walked. So: If Christ lives in you, shouldn't people feel His presence when they're in your presence? If you're on the church board, shouldn't the church be blessed? Shouldn't you be a change agent solving problems and helping the church grow? The church isn't perfect. Nobody said it was. It's a hospital, not an Ivy League club. But whatever is wrong with the church is man's doing, not God's. When God is behind even the smallest thing it becomes mighty; it must succeed because His power is absolute, unchanging, and available! It's time to "use God's mighty weapons...to knock down the strongholds" (2 Corinthians 10:4 NLT). It's time to force the issue by telling the Devil to take his hands off everything that concerns you! Jesus said, "All authority...has been given to me...therefore go" (Matthew 28:18-19 NIV). He has given you the power—use it!

PRAYER

Father, when I look in the mirror, I realize that every time I come up against something, the LAST thing I think of is to come directly to You. I'm always looking for someone with more faith than I have, to pray and believe on my behalf. I know I need to come to You boldly, and with the measure of faith You have given to me. Please help me to take this step of courage.

_____

_____

_____

_____

GOD'S PART

Lord, I know that I can't do Your part, and You won't do mine. So I trust you to:

_____

_____

_____

_____

MY PART

_____

_____

_____

_____

> You have given me Your Word and surrounded me with Your people, so that I can learn to stand on my own spiritual feet and come to You directly. And that's how I know, that of all the people in my life, You love me most!

57

"NOW" FAITH

"Now faith is the substance of things hoped for."

HEBREWS 11:1 NKJV

When you're in the middle of a crisis, what you really believe manifests itself in your words, attitude, and actions. When Lazarus died and his sister Martha said, "Lord, if you had been here, my brother would not have died" (John 11:21 NCV), she was voicing past-tense faith. When Jesus said, "[Lazarus] will...live again" (John 11:23 NCV) and she replied, "I know that he will...live...in the resurrection" (John 11:24 NCV), that was future-tense faith. And when she said, "Even now God will give you anything you ask" (John 11:22 NCV), she was demonstrating "now" faith, which is present tense. As believers, the Bible tells us not to "look at the things which are seen, but at the things which are not seen (2 Corinthians 4:18 NKJV). "Now" faith stakes its claim on "something...even if we do not see it" (Hebrews 11:1 NCV). Paul says, "We walk by faith, not by sight" (2 Corinthians 5:7 NKJV). Too often we base our feelings on what we see, instead of what God says in His Word. But as Jon Walker writes: "When we believe that reality is confined to what we see, we become trapped into thinking the only truth is what we see. We become prisoners of our own perceptions; we cease walking in faith... For those who walk by faith, appearances are never the ultimate reality...Reality extends beyond what you can see...the things we do not see are eternal [time and circumstance do not diminish or alter them] (See 2 Corinthians 4:18 NIV). Even though things may appear bad, God is working things out for our good (See Romans 8:28 NIV). He knows how the story ends, so fix your eyes on the unseen and not on what you see."

PRAYER

Father, today I am in crisis mode. I've no idea how I will get through this situation or what the outcome will be. All I can see are obstacles. Teach me to give You the reins and to stand in faith believing You for those things I have asked You for instead of trying to make them happen myself. Thank you.

_____
_____
_____
_____

GOD'S PART

Lord, I know that I can't do Your part, and You won't do mine. So I trust you to:

_____
_____
_____
_____

MY PART

_____
_____
_____
_____

I don't have to wait a week to pray about anything. You have given me "now" faith so that I can come to You at this very moment. And that's how I know, that of all the people in my life, You love me most!

HAVING DONE ALL, STAND IN FAITH WITH PATIENCE

58

THE VOICE OF FEAR

"Fear not; stand still [firm, confident,
undismayed]...He will work for you today."

EXODUS 14:13 AMPC

*I*f you're battling fear today, listen to these words from the God Who loves you, protects you, and promises to be with you: (1) When there seems to be no way out, He says, "Fear not; stand still (firm, confident, undismayed) and see the [deliverance] of the Lord which He will work for you today." Notice the words, "He will work for you today." Start looking for evidence of His hand at work in your situation; that's how your faith grows. (2) When the problem looks too big, He says, "Be strong, courageous, and firm; fear not nor be in terror before them, for it is the Lord your God Who goes with you; He will not fail you or forsake you" (Deuteronomy 31:6 AMPC). Stop and remind yourself whose company you're in. The One "Who goes with you" has never lost a battle, and He will win this one. (3) When you feel like you can't cope anymore, He says, "Do not look around you...and be dismayed, for I am your God. I will strengthen and harden you to difficulties" (Isaiah 41:10 AMPC). Notice the words "harden you to difficulties." God usually doesn't lift us out of the problem, He takes us through it and toughens us up. (4) When you lose your peace of mind, He says: "Do not fret or have any anxiety about anything, but in every circumstance...continue to make your wants known to God. And God's peace...which transcends all understanding shall garrison and mount guard over your hearts and minds" (Philippians 4:6-7 AMPC). Don't listen to the voice of fear. God is with you today!

PRAYER

Father, I have been working on letting Your voice be the only one I hear—especially over the self-talk that goes on in my head. I'm learning that I can trust You. And though I've let You down, You've always been faithful to me. Today I choose to not fear.

_____
_____
_____
_____

GOD'S PART

Lord, I know that I can't do Your part, and You won't do mine. So I trust you to:

_____
_____
_____
_____

151

MY PART

_____
_____
_____
_____

You tell me to have faith...to be of good courage. And I know You wouldn't direct me to do something without giving me the power to do it. And that's how I know, that of all the people in my life, You love me most!

59

STRENGTHEN YOUR FAITH

"You have...enlarged me when I was in distress."

PSALM 4:1 AMPC

*W*hen God wants to make you a bigger person, He does it through "distress." The way to build stronger muscle is to lift more weight. Now when a muscle is put under stress, you groan. But if you persist, that muscle grows stronger and what you were groaning about last week you are smiling about this week. Who said the Christian life was supposed to be easy? Not God! His Word compares it to a battlefield, not a bed of roses. "Endure hardship, as a good soldier" (2 Timothy 2:3 NKJV). Satan's number one target is your faith! Jesus said to Peter, "Satan has asked for you, that he may sift you as wheat. But I have prayed for you, that your faith should not fail" (Luke 22:31-32 NKJV). In the same way you separate wheat from chaff, Satan wants to separate you from your faith. Not only did Peter survive this attack, he grew through it and wrote: "Beloved, do not think it strange concerning the fiery trial which is to try you, as though some strange thing happened to you" (1 Peter 4:12 NKJV). Because we tend to be shocked when trials come our way, Peter deals with our attitude toward attack. He wants us to know how to think when we're under attack, to understand the appropriateness of the battle we are in. Satan may attack your health, but he's after your faith. He may attack your finances, but he's after your faith. If he can destroy your confidence in God and His Word, he wins—and you lose. So, the word for you today is "Strengthen your faith."

PRAYER

Lord, when I look back on my life, I see that the times I was in the most distress were the times when I became stronger and relied more on You. I want to be able to endure when hardships come into my life and not give up because I know You are always working things out for my good.

_____

_____

_____

_____

GOD'S PART

Lord, I know that I can't do Your part, and You won't do mine. So I trust you to:

_____

_____

_____

_____

153

MY PART

_____

_____

_____

_____

You never turn Your back on me. You always have a way out. And You give me just enough grace, so that my faith in You grows with every challenge. And that's how I know, that of all the people in my life, You love me most!

60

KEEP BELIEVING GOD!

"Faith is the assurance...of things [we] hope for...
the proof of things [we] do not see."

HEBREWS 11:1 AMPC

*A*re you praying yet nothing seems to be happening? Real faith knows God's promises and stands on them regardless. Listen, "Everyone who partakes only of milk is unskilled in the word" (Hebrews 5:13 NKJV). How skillful are you in the Scriptures? Have you found the promises that deal with your particular situation? Are you standing on them? When you pray do you conclude that if you don't feel something your prayers didn't work? If the circumstances don't change immediately, do you say, "I guess God isn't going to answer me?" Never speak words that contradict God. Satan can't read your mind, but he can hear your words! For 20 years Abraham kept repeating God's promise. Now when you're childless and 100, telling people you're going to be the "father of nations" can raise a few eyebrows! Circumstances mocked him. Reason defied him. Even his wife laughed. But he believed the God, "who calls those things which are not as though they are" (See Romans 4:17 KJV). This is not mind-over-matter or flaky theology; it's just doubting your doubts and still believing the God who cannot lie! When Jesus touched the blind man and then asked him what he could see, he replied, "I see men as trees, walking" (Mark 8:24 KJV). Did the man give up? Did Jesus quit in discouragement? No. He laid hands on him again, and this time he was completely healed. Keep going back to the source. Some answers come quickly and some slowly. Your fixed position must be—keep believing God.

PRAYER

Father, so many times when I need to pray, I stop in my tracks because I haven't taken the time to study Your Word to know which Scripture(s) to stand on. I'm expecting You or some other prayer warrior to get me out of the ditch. Please help me to not be intimidated by Your Word and to learn to discover it on my own.

_____

_____

_____

_____

GOD'S PART

Lord, I know that I can't do Your part, and You won't do mine. So I trust you to:

_____

_____

_____

_____

MY PART

_____

_____

_____

_____

There are times when You answer quickly and there are other times when I must wait patiently for the answer to come. But You are always on time—You are never late! And that's how I know, of all the people in my life, You love me most!

61

HOW LONG WILL THIS ATTACK LAST?

"Having done all...stand."

EPHESIANS 6:13 NKJV

The size of the prize determines the severity of the fight. The enemy knows your vulnerabilities and he'll push you to your limits. Listen: "Blessed is the man who endures...when he has been approved, he will receive the crown" (James 1:12 NKJV). "Approved" means victory qualifies you for greater things. "Endures" means your staying power is being tested. So, "having done all...stand." You say, "How long will this attack last?" The Prince of Darkness hindered Daniel's prayers for twenty-one days (See Daniel 10:13 NKJV). Goliath defied the armies of Israel forty days and nights (See 1 Samuel 17). Your enemy is relentless; you must be, too. "You have need of endurance, so that after you have done the will of God, you may receive the promise" (Hebrews 10:36 NKJV). David didn't get into trouble with Bathsheba until he left the battlefield. It's the safest place to be. So, stay there, keep fighting and God will come to your aid. When Joshua needed extra time to defeat his enemies, the sun stood still. God was saying, "As long as the sun doesn't go down you won't go down either, for the same power that's holding up the sun is holding you up too." Jesus healed people in different ways. Some He spoke to, others He touched. One day He told ten lepers to go and show themselves to the priest. And the Bible says: "As they went, they were cleansed" (Luke 17:14 NKJV). Faith doesn't demand details, it just keeps moving obediently forward, believing God for the right result!

PRAYER

Lord, You know me better than anyone. You know that sometimes I jump way ahead of You, and other times I refuse to take the path You have put in front of me. When that happens, I give in and fail instantly. Help me to see that by using all the tools that You've given me, I can come through any trial with Your help.

_____
_____
_____
_____

GOD'S PART

Lord, I know that I can't do Your part, and You won't do mine. So I trust you to:

_____
_____
_____
_____

MY PART

_____
_____
_____
_____

"Through" is such a beautiful word. It means that I don't have to stay stuck or under attack forever. God wants to bring me THROUGH! And that's how I know, that of all the people in my life, You love me most!

62

DEVELOPING STRONG ROOTS

"Let your roots grow down into him and draw up nourishment
from him. See that you go on growing in the Lord."

COLOSSIANS 2:7 TLB

*F*aith grows only in the soil of adversity! When young plants get too much rain, even a short drought can kill them. Why? Because it was too easy! During frequent rains, they didn't have to push their roots deeper into the soil in search of water; they didn't develop any strength, so they have a weak, shallow root system, they die quickly. How's your 'root system?' When stress and adversity enter your life, do you hold up or fold up? Do you find yourself thinking God has abandoned you or do you start doubting Him? Look out! Ease is your enemy! When you become too comfortable, you stop 'digging deeper' in the Word. You allow others to spoon-feed you rather than develop your own personal relationship with God through prayer and Bible study. Thank God for the rain, but you have to develop a 'root system' that will sustain you in the hard times. Remember, your old friend the devil has now become your adversary and he's out to get you (See 1 Peter 5:8 NKJV). You won't prepare for a fight you're not expecting, so, Paul says, "Put on God's complete armor, that you may be able to resist and stand your ground on the evil day [of danger] and, having done all [the crisis demands], to stand [firmly in your place]" (Ephesians 6:13 AMPC). Now, there's something to think about!

PRAYER

Father, I must learn to stand on my own two spiritual legs. I must put time and energy into my relationship with You in order to grow and know that You are faithful. Please forgive me for trying to take the easy way out. That's not Your best—and I want Your best!

GOD'S PART

Lord, I know that I can't do Your part, and You won't do mine. So I trust you to:

MY PART

I can't delegate the task of developing my relationship with God to someone else. I have to invest myself into the process. And that's how I know, that of all the people in my life, You love me most!

FAMILY

63

GIVE YOUR CHILDREN THESE FOUR THINGS

"Bring them...and I will bless them."

GENESIS 48:9 NKJV

*G*ive your children these four things: (1) Instruction. "Do not forget the things your eyes have seen or let them slip from your heart as long as you live. Teach them to your children" (Deuteronomy 4:9 NIV). It is not the responsibility of the government or the school system to instill character and convictions in your child; it's your job! And God will hold you accountable for it. (2) Correction. "Discipline your children while there is hope" (Proverbs 19:18 NLT). Children who know how far they can go are relieved of a great burden. Knowing your authority will stand gives them security. When they learn that NO, really means NO, they'll be able to say it to others, and to their own impulses. (3) Blessing. "Joseph said to his father, 'They are my sons'...And he [Jacob] said...'Bring them to me and I will bless them'" (Genesis 48:8-9 NKJV). Old Testament parents laid hands on their children because they believed the blessing of God was transferable. If nobody did this for you then start a new tradition, for with God's blessing comes peace, long life, and prosperity (See Deuteronomy 28 NKJV). That's why the enemy has attacked you so often; he's trying to break the link through which the blessing of God comes. Don't let him. (4) Example. A great preacher once looked into the crib of his infant son and prayed: "Lord, if ever You made a man, make me one now. Let my life, my example and my prayers mold him into someone You can use. And, Lord, let me die twenty-four hours before I say or do anything that would cause him to stumble."

PRAYER
Father, I want to raise my children to be healthy, productive members of society. Most of all, I want them to love and serve You. Help me to be the parent I need to be, to not be afraid to discipline my children and hold them accountable for their actions.

_____
_____
_____
_____

GOD'S PART
Lord, I know that I can't do Your part, and You won't do mine. So I trust you to:

_____
_____
_____
_____

MY PART

_____
_____
_____
_____

> Your Word tells me to discipline my children while there is hope. You want my children to live a long life and to prosper in all they do. And that's how I know, that of all the people in my life, You love me most!

64

WHAT PAUL PRAYED FOR

"We have not stopped praying for you."

COLOSSIANS 1:9 NIV

*W*hen it came to those he loved, notice what Paul prayed for: (1) That they would understand the will of God. "Ask God to fill you with the knowledge of his will through all wisdom and understanding" (Colossians 1:9 NIV). Rome was not an easy place to be a Christian, yet Paul wrote: "Everyone has heard about your obedience" (Romans 16:19 NIV). Obedience to God's will should be your number one priority. When your name is mentioned, no one should have any doubt as to the level of your commitment to Jesus. (2) That their lives would be pleasing to God. "That you may live a life worthy of the Lord and may please him in every way" (Colossians 1:10 NIV). When you stand before God to be rewarded you won't hear the words "well said," or "well planned," but, "Well done, good and faithful servant" (Matthew 25:21 NKJV). (3) That they would prosper in the work God had given them. "Bearing fruit in every good work" (Colossians 1:10 NIV). Nothing brings joy to the heart of a parent like seeing their child succeed. And God feels the same way about you. (4) That they would persevere by drawing on His strength. "Being strengthened with all power according to his glorious might so that you may have great endurance" (Colossians 1:11 NIV). Like a light bulb, you depend on power from another source. So, unless you stay connected to God, you'll be spiritually weak. (5) That they would praise God. "Giving joyful thanks to the Father, who has qualified you to share in the inheritance of his holy people" (Colossians 1:12 NIV). In other words, live with an attitude of gratitude and a heart of praise.

PRAYER

Lord, I want my life to be pleasing in Your sight. Help me to be obedient to Your Word and put it into practice each day of my life. When I stand before You, I want to hear the words, "Well done good and faithful servant."

_____

_____

_____

_____

GOD'S PART

Lord, I know that I can't do Your part, and You won't do mine. So I trust you to:

_____

_____

_____

_____

MY PART

_____

_____

_____

_____

165

> I know You want me to succeed and that prayer is my direct connection to You. And that's how I know, that of all the people in my life, You love me most!

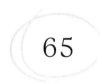

65

WHEN YOUR MATE DOESN'T SHARE YOUR FAITH

"If a woman has a husband who is not a believer..."

1 CORINTHIANS 7:13 NIV

*L*iving with an unbelieving mate is both a challenge and an opportunity. It's a challenge because believers and unbelievers see life differently. And it's an opportunity because God can use you to close the gap and win them to Christ. But for that to take place you must make two commitments: (1) Commit yourself to the goal of their salvation. (2) Commit yourself to your own growth through loving them and living with them. Once you've committed, you're ready for this practical and helpful counsel. Remember the unbeliever's spiritual limitations. "Therefore, if anyone is in Christ, he is a new creation; old things have passed away; all things have become new" (2 Corinthians 5:17 NKJV). Only when they're "in Christ" can they be a "new creation." Only then will "the old" go! The old will dominate until they receive the new. "That which is born of the flesh is flesh; and that which is born of the Spirit is spirit" (John 3:6 NKJV). Remember, the unbeliever suffers from spiritual birth defects they can't overcome until the new birth corrects them. "The flesh is hostile toward God; for it does not subject itself to the law of God, for it is not even able to do so and those who are in the flesh cannot please God" (Romans 8:7-8 NASB). If they don't love God's Word, prayer and church like you do, it's because they're controlled by the flesh and are "not even able" to. So have realistic expectations. Remember what you were like B.C. (Before Christ)? Be patient, loving and kind while God does His work in them.

PRAYER

Lord, I want to my mate to share my faith and serve You. Often it is a challenge because we see things so differently. Help me be patient and kind toward my him/her while you do Your work in his/her life.

_____

_____

_____

_____

GOD'S PART

Lord, I know that I can't do Your part, and You won't do mine. So I trust you to:

_____

_____

_____

_____

MY PART

_____

_____

_____

_____

> I know that by Your Spirit you can work in the heart of my mate and that You will never give up on them because You never give up on me. And that's how I know, that of all the people in my life, You love me most!

66

GETTING ALONG WITH EACH OTHER (1)

"You must get along with each other..."

1 CORINTHIANS 1:10 MSG

If you're serious about restoring a broken relationship: (1) Before you talk to the other person, talk to God. He can change their heart, your heart, or both hearts. It's amazing how different you feel when you've prayed. Often the conflict is rooted in unmet needs. Any time you expect human beings to meet needs only God can meet, you're in trouble. "What causes...quarrels among you?...You desire but do not have...you covet but you cannot get what you want...because you do not ask God" (James 4:1-2 NIV). Instead of looking to God, you look to people, then you get angry when they fail you. God says, "Why don't you come to me first?" (2) Arrange to talk to them one-on-one. Even though you've been offended, God expects you to make the first move: "Go and be reconciled to that person" (Matthew 5:24 NLT). We say, "Time heals." Not necessarily; sometimes it just causes wounds to fester. Taking control of the situation reduces the damage. Plus, bitterness only hurts your fellowship with God and keeps your prayers from being answered. Job's friends reminded him, "You are only hurting yourself with your anger" (Job 18:4 GNT). (3) Timing is all-important. Don't try to mend a relationship when you're tired, rushed, or will be interrupted. And don't do it "on the fly." The time and effort you're willing to put into restoring it indicates the value you place on the relationship. So, do it when you're both at your best. You say, "I'm not sure I can do it." Yes, you can; God "has given us this ministry of restoring relationships" (2 Corinthians 5:18 GWT).

PRAYER

I want my relationship with _____ to be mended.
I no longer want to hold unforgiveness in my heart toward them.
Help me to not expect _____ to meet a need in
my life that only You can meet or fill a void that only You can fill.

_____

_____

_____

_____

GOD'S PART

Lord, I know that I can't do Your part, and You won't do mine.
So I trust you to:

_____

_____

_____

_____

MY PART

_____

_____

_____

_____

No matter how many times I fail You're always
there to pick me up. You help me understand the
importance of forgiveness. And that's how I know,
that of all the people in my life, You love me most!

67

GETTING ALONG WITH EACH OTHER (2)

"You must get along with each other..."

1 CORINTHIANS 1:10 MSG

Getting along with each other requires more than compliance, it calls for cooperation. So: (1) Validate the other person's feelings! Never try to talk someone out of how they "feel." Listen without being defensive, and nod that you understand, even when you don't agree. Feelings aren't always true or logical, but until they're validated you won't get anywhere. David said, "When my...feelings were hurt, I was...stupid" (Psalm 73:21-22 GNT). We all act badly when we're hurt. But Solomon says, "A person's wisdom yields patience; it is to one's glory to overlook an offense" (Proverbs 19:11 NIV). When you are willing to empathize with someone's feelings it says, "I care about our relationship more than our differences; you matter to me." Sure, it's a sacrifice to patiently absorb somebody's anger, especially when it's unfounded. But remember, that's what Jesus does for you! (2) Confess your part. Jesus said, "First get rid of the log in your own eye; then you will see well enough to deal with the speck in your friend's eye" (Matthew 7:5 NLT). Since we all have blind spots, get a friend to help you evaluate your attitudes and actions before meeting with the other person. Ask God, "Am I part of the problem? Am I unrealistic, insensitive, or too sensitive?" Confession is a powerful tool! When you can admit your own flaws, it defuses the other person's anger because they're expecting you to be defensive. Don't make excuses or shift blame, just acknowledge your part and make your peace.

PRAYER

I know I need to learn to listen without getting defensive or angry. I need You to show me when I am wrong and when I am part of the problem. Help me to offer forgiveness to _____ and to ask for forgiveness when I am the one who has done wrong.

_____

_____

_____

_____

GOD'S PART

Lord, I know that I can't do Your part, and You won't do mine. So I trust you to:

_____

_____

_____

_____

MY PART

_____

_____

_____

_____

> You are the ultimate example of unconditional love and forgiveness—You've forgiven me a million times for my mistakes. And that's how I know, that of all the people in my life, You love me most!

FRIENDS

68

"AS-IS"

"Bearing with one another."

COLOSSIANS 3:13 NASB

Have you ever been in a discount store where merchandise is labeled "slightly irregular," or "purchase as is"? They don't tell you where the flaw is. And once you buy it you can't return it. Well, in case you haven't noticed, we all live in the "as is" department. Stop and think about the people in your life. They're a mixed bag of strengths and weaknesses, virtues and vices, right? If you're looking for perfection, you're in the wrong store. What's the point? It's this: The only way to have a successful relationship with someone is to love and accept them "as is." Don't buy into the myth that most folks are "normal" except the ones in your life. Based on that idea, relationships are an endless quest to fix others, control them, or pretend they are something they're not. Thomas Merton said, "Love is letting those we love be perfectly themselves, and not twisting them to fit our own image. Otherwise we love only the reflection of ourselves we see in them." A hallmark of spiritual maturity is acknowledging that nobody is perfect and committing to love them in spite of it. Paul writes: "Be gentle and forbearing with one another and, if one has a difference (a grievance or complaint) against another, readily pardoning each other; even as the Lord has [freely] forgiven you, so you must also [forgive]" (Colossians 3:13 AMPC). To love someone "as is" means to focus on their areas of strength and support them in their areas of struggle. "What about their flaws?" you say. "Love covers a multitude of sins" (1 Peter 4:8 NLT).

PRAYER

Lord, I know that we are all a mixed bag of strengths and weaknesses and that we all come into relationships with our fair share of baggage. Help me to be patient and to show love and kindness to my friends and to forgive them as You have forgiven me.

GOD'S PART

Lord, I know that I can't do Your part, and You won't do mine. So I trust you to:

MY PART

175

Even though I have flaws You accept me as-is.
When I say or do the wrong thing You don't get
angry with me. And that's how I know, that of
all the people in my life, You love me most!

69

SHOW GRACE

"Forgiveness...in accordance with the riches of...God's grace."

EPHESIANS 1:7 NIV

*E*ver notice how quickly we judge somebody else's shortcomings while making all kinds of allowance for our own? Paul talks about "the riches of...grace" that God lavished on us. But we strain that grace when we refuse to extend it to others. Jesus said, "When you stand praying, if you hold anything against anyone, forgive them, so that your Father...may forgive you" (Mark 11:25 NIV). You don't get to decide which offenses you'll forgive and which ones you'll keep holding over somebody's head. We are commanded to "act justly and to love mercy" (Micah 6:8 NIV). That means we must pursue it and make it our goal. Don't say, "I'll forgive him when he proves he deserves it." Biblical forgiveness isn't conditional, can't be earned, isn't deserved, and you can't bargain for it. Jesus said, "Give as freely as you have received!" (Matthew 10:8 NLT). "If I forgive her, she'll have gotten away with it." You're not letting anybody get away with anything, because even when you've forgiven the offender there's still a penalty to be paid. It's just not your job to enforce it. "If I forgive him, he'll keep hurting me." Forgiveness doesn't mean the relationship always stays the same. It takes time to rebuild trust and make sure repentance is genuine. In fact, if the offense is abusive or puts you in danger—forgive but maintain a safe distance. "If I forgive her, she's free to hurt me again." The truth is, she's free to do it again anyway, just like you're free to show grace even when the offender doesn't ask or show any sign of repentance.

PRAYER

Lord, I know I can be quick to judge other people, while I overlook the shortcomings in my own life. Help me to release any bitterness that is in my heart toward others. I want to give them the grace and mercy that You have so freely given to me.

GOD'S PART

Lord, I know that I can't do Your part, and You won't do mine. So I trust you to:

MY PART

There is no end to Your grace and mercy.
There is no place I can go to outrun Your love
for me. And that's how I know, that of all
the people in my life, You love me most!

70

DOES THIS PERSON BELONG IN MY LIFE?

"Can two walk together, unless they are agreed?"

AMOS 3:3 NKJV

*A*toxic relationship is like a limb with gangrene: Unless you amputate it, the infection can spread and kill you. Without the courage to cut off what refuses to heal, you'll end up losing a lot more. Your personal growth—and in some cases your healing—will only be expedited by establishing relationships with the right people. Maybe you've heard the story about the scorpion who asked the frog to carry him across the river because he couldn't swim. "I'm afraid you'll sting me," replied the frog. The scorpion smiled reassuringly and said, "Of course I won't. If I did that, we'd both drown!" So, the frog agreed, and the scorpion hopped on his back. Wouldn't you know it: Halfway across the river the scorpion stung him! As they began to sink the frog lamented, "You promised you wouldn't sting me. Why'd you do it?" The scorpion replied, "I can't help it. It's my nature!" Until God changes the other person's nature, they have the power to affect and infect you. For example, when you feel passionately about something, but others don't, it's like trying to dance a foxtrot with someone who only knows how to waltz. You picked the wrong dance partner! Don't get tied up with someone who doesn't share your values and God-given goals. Some issues can be corrected through counseling, prayer, teaching, and leadership. But you can't teach someone to care; if they don't care they'll pollute your environment, kill your productivity, and break your rhythm with constant complaints. That's why it's important to pray and ask God, "Does this person belong in my life?"

PRAYER

Lord, for some reason I find myself drawn to toxic people. Something in me wants to fix them. I know that only You can mend the hurt in their lives and break the chains that bind them. I ask You to help me let go and release them to Your care.

_____
_____
_____
_____

GOD'S PART

Lord, I know that I can't do Your part, and You won't do mine. So I trust you to:

_____
_____
_____
_____

MY PART

_____
_____
_____
_____

> You are a friend who sticks closer than a brother—and I can have no better friend than You. And that's how I know, that of all the people in my life, You love me most!

71

DON'T BE UNDERMINED

"Bad company corrupts good character."

1 CORINTHIANS 15:33 NIV

*G*od told His people, "I will not drive them out before you; but they shall be thorns in your side…and…be a snare to you" (Judges 2:3 NKJV). Was God being uncharitable? No, He just understood that if His people hung out with the Canaanites, they'd pick up the habits, seek their approval, live by their values, and end up worshipping their gods! That's why He laid down His law so clearly! John Maxwell says, "You'll acquire the vices and virtues of your closest associates. The fragrance of their lives will pervade yours." He's right! You can tell yourself that a bad relationship won't hurt you; or that your good will rub off on them. But who are you kidding? If you put on white gloves, go into your back yard and pick up dirt, the dirt won't get glovey but the gloves will get dirty. Right? Wake up! A toxic relationship is like a malignant cell; you may be okay for a while, but if left unchecked, eventually it'll rob you of your health, and maybe even your life. Cervantes, who wrote Don Quixote, said, "Tell me your company, and I'll tell you who you are." Take another look at the influences in your life today, for they're doing 2 things: (1) molding you; (2) motivating you. If a constant drip can wear away a rock, then the wrong influences can undermine you little by little. But you're not a rock, you can move!

PRAYER

Lord, I have been hanging around with the wrong people. I have allowed them to influence my life in negative ways and I've violated my own values. I come to You today and ask You to forgive me and to give me the strength to cut them out of my life and turn back to You.

_____

_____

_____

_____

GOD'S PART

Lord, I know that I can't do Your part, and You won't do mine. So I trust you to:

_____

_____

_____

_____

MY PART

_____

_____

_____

_____

Your love for me is the only validation I need in my life. You care for me and only want what is best for me. And that's how I know, that of all the people in my life, You love me most!

DIFFICULT RELATIONSHIPS

72

STAYING WHEN YOU FEEL LIKE LEAVING (1)

"Humans must not pull apart what God has put together."

MARK 10:9 CEB

*N*ot every relationship can be saved. When physical, mental, or emotional abuse threatens your child's safety, or your own, you may be forced to leave. Failing to do so could lead to tragedy. But where a workable resolution can be found, a troubled relationship can become a source of shared joy and fulfillment. Here are some keys to make staying worthwhile: Adopt God's perspective on sin—yours and your spouse's. One of the major problems is the way we classify sin—especially our partner's. You're understandably overwrought and anxious because they're incorrigible and selfish. They're the willful sinner—you're the offended saint. They need a major overhaul, and you're responsible to see they get it. Things like being critical, nagging, and controlling seem like small things compared to a spouse who swears, drinks, and visits porn sites. From God's perspective, sin is sin—yours and theirs! It's all harmful to relationships. Stop "classifying" sin and try to discover the relationship-transforming power of handling the situation the way Jesus taught. "How can you say to your brother, 'Let me take the speck out of your eye,' when all the time there is a plank in your own eye? You hypocrite; first take the plank out of your own eye, and then you will see clearly to remove the speck from your brother's eye" (Matthew 7:4-5 NIV). You'll be amazed at how God will cause your spouse to acknowledge and deal with "their" problem when you get honest and deal with "yours"!

PRAYER
Lord, I know that you brought _____ into my life. You have joined us together, but right now, I want to walk away. Help me to take a deep breath and not add fuel to the fire by overreacting. Help me to show love and forgiveness to my mate and to find a way to work through our problems.

_____
_____
_____
_____

GOD'S PART
Lord, I know that I can't do Your part, and You won't do mine. So I trust you to:

_____
_____
_____
_____

MY PART

_____
_____
_____
_____

When I am wrong You hold the mirror of Your Word up so that I can see my own shortcomings, but You never walk away or desert me. And that's how I know, that of all the people in my life, You love me most!

73

STAYING WHEN YOU FEEL LIKE LEAVING (2)

"In order that Satan might not outwit us."

2 CORINTHIANS 2:11 NIV

ecognize who the real enemy of your marriage is. On those days when you think, "I can't spend another moment in this relationship," it's easy to lose perspective and focus on the wrong things. Marriage was God's idea. He planned it as the foundation of His earthly kingdom. That makes marriage one of Satan's prime targets. It's why he poisoned the perspective and confused the thinking of the first couple. He deceived Adam into believing that Eve was his problem, blaming the fiasco on her (See Genesis 3:12 NKJV). But both were deceived by "the father of lies" (John 8:44 NLT). Satan knew he could undermine God's plan by driving a wedge between the first couple, creating antagonism, blame, and self-interest. And his methods haven't changed. It's why we "keep tabs" on each other's shortcomings, identifying our mate as the problem and refusing to show grace. Paul helps us understand how to overcome Satan's strategy. "I have forgiven in the sight of Christ...in order that Satan might not outwit us...we are not unaware of his schemes" (2 Corinthians 2:10-11 NIV). Then he counsels us further by saying that "love...doesn't keep score of the sins of others" (1 Corinthians 13:4-5 MSG). That doesn't mean love lives in denial, but that it chooses to practice self-denial! So rather than keeping score of your spouse's worst qualities, choose to look for their best ones and show your appreciation. Nothing melts resentment and hardness like expressing appreciation for each other.

PRAYER

Lord, I don't want to give up on my marriage, I want to stay and make things right. Help me not to see my mate as the problem and focus only on what they have done wrong. I know I need to show grace in this situation, and I need Your help to do it.

_____

_____

_____

_____

GOD'S PART

Lord, I know that I can't do Your part, and You won't do mine. So I trust you to:

_____

_____

_____

_____

MY PART

_____

_____

_____

_____

Marriage is Your idea and You want me to have
a relationship that is founded on love, trust,
and respect. And that's how I know, that of all
the people in my life, You love me most!

74

STAYING WHEN YOU FEEL LIKE LEAVING (3)

"Pray then like this...your will be done."

MATTHEW 6:9-10 ESV

*H*ere are another two helpful keys to resolving marriage conflict: (1) Let God direct your prayers. Prayer can be closed-ended or open-ended. When we think that our perspective is the only accurate one, we pray closed-ended prayers calling on God to solve the problem our way, believing it's the only correct way. But closed-ended praying produces two problems. First, it locks us into rigid thinking and blinds us to other perspectives. Second, it keeps us from seeing God's perspective, the one that can heal and restore the relationship. Open-ended praying asks God to solve the problem His way. "Pray then like this...your will be done." Ask God to reveal His will to you both, wait until He does, then pray accordingly. The Bible says: "This is the confidence we have in approaching God: that if we ask anything according to his will, he hears us. And if we know that he hears us...we know that we have what we asked of him" (1 John 5:14-15 NIV). (2) Remove the conditions from your love. Sound difficult? Love is a biblical command, not an arbitrary emotion. God's not asking you to feel warm and fuzzy, He's asking you to act in a loving way. Wouldn't that be hypocritical? No, it's rising above resentment, hurt, and fear, and practicing real faith. It means asking yourself: "If I were loving unconditionally right now, what would I be doing? How would I be responding to my spouse?" Then do it. The Bible says, "Love never fails" (1 Corinthians 13:8 NIV). You can lovingly act your way into a new way of feeling for both you and your spouse.

PRAYER

Lord, I feel like the conflict never ends no matter what I do. Show me how to move beyond our problems and see things from another perspective. I love my mate and I want to work this out, but I need Your help to do it.

_____

_____

_____

_____

GOD'S PART

Lord, I know that I can't do Your part, and You won't do mine. So I trust you to:

_____

_____

_____

_____

MY PART

_____

_____

_____

_____

When I feel like giving up Your love surrounds
me. When I feel there is no hope, I hear Your voice
say—I am with you. And that's how I know, that
of all the people in my life, You love me most!

75

STAYING WHEN YOU FEEL LIKE LEAVING (4)

"Pile your troubles on God's shoulders."

PSALM 55:22 MSG

Give your marriage to God. The last word on the matter must be God's Word! Seeking professional help is a good thing. But until you've transferred ownership of your marriage into God's hands, you haven't exercised your best option. You say, "What does giving my marriage over to God mean in practical terms?" It means two things: (1) You stop calling the shots— that's God's job. And you must get out of His way so that He can do His work unhindered. Your self-interest and need to control must bow to His will. As long as you insist on "being right" and "straightening out" your spouse, you will remain part of the problem. On the other hand, when you give the problem to God, He—not you—has a problem to work on! (2) You learn how to "walk by faith, not by sight" (2 Corinthians 5:7 NKJV). When things feel out of control you will want to resume ownership of the problem. Don't do it, or the result will be more of what doesn't work. Renew your decision to allow God to have control and work in both of your hearts. "Walk by faith," not by feelings. The Psalmist puts it this way: "Pile your troubles on God's shoulders—he'll carry your load, he'll help you out." When you trust God to handle it, three things happen: (a) You experience peace; (b) your partner's resistance will likely diminish because you're no longer stirring the pot; (c) God goes to work: "He who began a good work in you [both] will bring it to completion" (Philippians 1:6 ESV).

PRAYER
Lord, today I turn my marriage over to You—I can't work it out, but You can. Help me set my feelings aside and trust You to guide us through these difficult waters. I will choose to walk in love and let You do the work that needs to be done in our lives.

_____
_____
_____
_____

GOD'S PART
Lord, I know that I can't do Your part, and You won't do mine. So I trust you to:

_____
_____
_____
_____

MY PART

_____
_____
_____
_____

191

> When I stop trying to control things and bring You into the picture, I feel the burden lift off my shoulders and peace come into my heart. And that's how I know, that of all the people in my life, You love me most!

76

FORGIVENESS

"Forgiving each other, just as...God forgave you."

EPHESIANS 4:32 NIV

The Bible says, "Be kind...forgiving each other...as...God forgave you." Kristin Armstrong says: "After you forgive...you get to walk out the process...it's a collaborative effort of God's power and your hard work. Letting go isn't always as simple as opening your tightly clenched fist, although deliverance sometimes is immediate. For example, some people quit smoking cold turkey, while others chew nicotine gum for years! Old habits die hard and letting go of resentment means: (a) Recommitting to your decision as many times as old thoughts of unforgiveness pop into your head. (b) Making peace with the space formerly occupied by bitterness, regret and thoughts of revenge until the Holy Spirit takes up full-time occupancy in the new digs! (c) Releasing old, toxic relationships and people whose only purpose is keeping your old wounds fresh. When people change around unchanging people, it makes them aware of their own need for change, and it scares them. (d) Just as your salvation is immediate yet you have to walk out your sanctification, the release of your forgiveness is immediate, but you have to walk out your healing. (e) Living a life free from the burden of resentment and the toxicity of unforgiveness is a choice followed by a series of choices. Each one becomes easier...as we move farther from our old ways and into the light...Paul said, 'It is for freedom that Christ has set us free' (Galatians 5:1 NIV) and every time we let something or someone go free, we receive freedom for ourselves in overflowing proportion. It's a time-tested, guaranteed spiritual principle backed by the promise of Scripture."

PRAYER

Lord, I know that you have forgiven me for all my wrongs, therefore I must forgive others. There are times when I forgive but then I take it back and rehearse it over and over in my mind. I want to let go of all the hurt I feel inside, and learn to LET GO and LET GOD.

_____
_____
_____
_____

GOD'S PART

Lord, I know that I can't do Your part, and You won't do mine. So I trust you to:

_____
_____
_____
_____

MY PART

_____
_____
_____
_____

I am amazed at Your never-ending love for me.
I am amazed at how You can forgive me over
and over again for the same offense and not
give up on me. And that's how I know, that of
all the people in my life, You love me most!

77

SET BOUNDARIES

"All you need to say is simply 'Yes' or 'No'."

MATTHEW 5:37 NIV

*W*hen does "a good thing" become "too much?" Can I help you, without hurting me? Can we share our lives, without me giving up mine? When do you truly need my help? When do I need to let go, and let you and God handle it? Finding the balance between "enough" and "too much" in relationships is a constant challenge and isn't easy. Especially when your role tends to be, "all things, at all times, to all people," and theirs is, "I'm helpless, you owe me, take care of me"; when you have no "no" and they have no "yes." Needing to be needed by needy people who always want someone to take care of them, puts the needy person in the driver's seat—and puts you over the edge. They are never happy, whatever you do. So, you do more to make them feel happier and yourself feel less guilty, and you end up in a double bind. They resent you for not giving enough, and you resent them for not appreciating what you give. Yet neither of you knows how to break the cycle. So, the relationship becomes what counselors call a "more-of-the-same" tangle where both parties resent and devalue the other, feeling stuck in a life-dominating trap you both fear to jettison. Marriages, families, friendships, workplaces, churches, and social groups get trapped in this "victim-rescuer" pattern where needy people and fixers become lock-stepped in a mutual dance they both "love to hate," but won't stop doing! Recognize yourself? If so, you're moving toward a healthier, less toxic relationship.

PRAYER

Father, I need You to help me set healthy boundaries in my life. I am a fixer, and it's hard for me to find the balance between caring for others and being used. I know I need to break the cycle of dependency and learn to say 'No' when people require too much of me.

_____

_____

_____

_____

GOD'S PART

Lord, I know that I can't do Your part, and You won't do mine. So I trust you to:

_____

_____

_____

_____

MY PART

_____

_____

_____

_____

When I move toward healthier and less toxic
relationships, I am free to be all You have
called me to be. You don't want me burdened
and sad. And that's how I know, that of all
the people in my life, You love me most!

STAYING CONNECTED

78

STAY CONNECTED

"I am the vine, you are the branches..."

JOHN 15:5 NKJV

*L*isten, "I am the vine, ye are the branches..." (John 15:5 NKJV). Until you really understand those words, you'll keep trying to do things that only God can do. Things like— blessing yourself, solving your own problems, answering your own prayers, and promoting your own ministry. Or worse, you'll try to cover up for God because He's not doing things quickly enough, and you're standing there like a substitute teacher trying to make Him look good through human efforts. Give it up; it can't be done! Jesus said, "I am the vine; ye are the branches..." All you have to do is stay connected! King Saul's greatest concern was his standing before the people. King David's greatest concern was his standing before God. What a difference! When was the last time you prayed, "Lord, make me better?" Most of the time we pray, "Lord, make me bigger." Listen, if you abide, you'll automatically abound! You've got to know where your help comes from, otherwise you'll waste your time chasing people who have no more power than you have. Jesus said, "...the Son can do nothing of himself..." (John 5:19 NKJV). Indeed, He never even bothered to try. We, on the other hand say, "Without Him I can do nothing," then we go out and act as if it all depends on us. If we succeed, nobody can live with us; if we fail, it's because He never gave us the assignment to begin with. Your success is in the Vine! Your business is in the Vine! Your future is in the Vine! All you have to do is stay connected!

PRAYER

Father, I know that in order to keep growing, I must stay connected to You and to Your Word. I can't answer my own prayers or fix things through human effort. I must rely completely on You Lord, because without You I can do nothing.

_____
_____
_____
_____

GOD'S PART

Lord, I know that I can't do Your part, and You won't do mine. So I trust you to:

_____
_____
_____
_____

MY PART

_____
_____
_____
_____

> You want me to stay connected to You because You are the source of my strength, my light in the darkness, and hope when I can't find my way. And that's how I know, that of all the people in my life, You love me most!

79

KEYS TO ANSWERED PRAYER

"Ask, and you will receive, that your joy may be full."

JOHN 16:24 NKJV

*I*f your prayers are not being answered, ask yourself: (1) How is my relationship with the Lord? "If I regard iniquity in my heart, the Lord will not hear me" (Psalm 66:18 KJV). Anything that adversely affects your relationship with God also affects your prayers. Friendship gives you favor; intimacy gives you access. Jesus said, "If you abide in Me, and My words abide in you, you will ask what you desire, and it shall be done for you" (John 15:7 NKJV). (2) How strong is my faith? "Without faith it is impossible to please Him, for he who comes to God must believe that He is...a rewarder of those who diligently seek Him" (Hebrews 11:6 NKJV). Notice three words: (a) "Believe." God's deepest longing is to be believed, regardless of emotion, or circumstance. (b) "Diligently." When you pray, put your heart and soul into it. Paul speaks of "laboring in prayer" (See Colossians 4:12 NKJV). (c) "Him." God is not some "force out there," He's your heavenly Father Who "knows that you need all these things" (Matthew 6:32 NKJV). Your highest priority should not be getting your needs met, it should be building your relationship with God. (3) Am I showing patience? "Until God's time finally came— how God tested his patience!" (Psalm 105:19 TLB). Joseph was tested by the very promise God gave him. Can't you hear Satan whisper, "I thought the dream said you were supposed to be prime minister; what are you doing in prison?" But it only looks like a prison; in reality, it's the birthplace of destiny. Joseph saw God's promise fulfilled—in God's time. And you will too!

PRAYER

Lord, I know that without faith it is impossible to please You, and that in order to get my prayers answered I must stand on Your Word and wait patiently for You to act. Today, I make a decision that having done all—I will stand. By faith I expect to see You turn things around in my life.

_____

_____

_____

_____

GOD'S PART

Lord, I know that I can't do Your part, and You won't do mine. So I trust you to:

_____

_____

_____

_____

MY PART

_____

_____

_____

_____

You are my heavenly Father, and I am Your child.
It is Your desire to answer my prayers according
to Your Word. And that's how I know, that of all
the people in my life, You love me most!

80

PRAYER

"Seek his face always."

1 CHRONICLES 16:11 NIV

A good relationship is based on being sensitive to the other person's needs, and to do that, you must make the relationship a priority and spend time together. The difference between "catching a few moments" with the Lord and spending quality time with Him is like the difference between driving through McDonald's and spending the evening at a fine restaurant. At McDonald's you drive up, shout into a microphone, and drive around to a window where they hand you a bag of food. In a fine restaurant you sit down, savor every bite in a relaxed atmosphere, and leave satisfied and nourished. Too many of us live on spiritual fast food and never experience the banquet God has for us. The Bible says, "Seek his face continually." Have you learned how to stay in God's presence and enjoy it? When it comes to prayer, we all face two challenges: (1) Lack of desire. We complain about lack of time, but the truth is we make time for what we truly care about and enjoy. If you want to build an effective prayer life you must be willing to forfeit some things. (2) We don't know how. Find a place with no distractions. Take your Bible and a notepad with you. Use a CD player with worship music to help you. Worship will change the atmosphere around you. Just do what works for you. And be patient! Sometimes it takes weeks or months before you develop a pattern, so stick with it—the rewards are worth it. And remember, prayer is a two-way street. It's not about seeing how much you can tell God; it's about learning to hear from Him as well.

PRAYER

Father, I want to learn to spend quality time with You and not rush into my day without talking to You first. I know when I forget to pray, things go wrong, and I lose my way. I want to know You more and I commit myself to making prayer a priority in my life.

_____

_____

_____

_____

GOD'S PART

Lord, I know that I can't do Your part, and You won't do mine. So I trust you to:

_____

_____

_____

_____

MY PART

_____

_____

_____

_____

When I step away from all distractions and allow myself to be still, I can hear Your still, small voice speaking to my heart. And that's how I know, that of all the people in my life, You love me most!

81

HOW IS YOUR RELATIONSHIP WITH GOD?

"I do not seek My own will but the will
of the Father who sent Me."

JOHN 5:30 NKJV

*T*hree things describe Christ's relationship with His Father: intimacy, dependency, and obedience. Today let's look at His dependency on God. "The Son can do nothing of Himself, but what He sees the Father do; for whatever He does, the Son also does in like manner" (John 5:19 NKJV). Jesus knew He couldn't do anything without His Father, so He didn't bother to try. We, on the other hand, sing, "Without Him I can do nothing," then go out and act like it all depends on us. If we succeed, we often become so conceited that nobody can stand us. And if we fail, it's usually because we collapsed under the weight of an assignment God didn't give us in the first place. Have you ever wondered why Jesus never struggled with insecurity or battled the fear of failure like we do? Because it never even occurred to Him that He couldn't do something which His Father had already assured Him He could do. When you know you have heard from God you can face any obstacle or enemy with confidence. God will never give you an assignment that does not require His wisdom and undergirding strength. Indeed, every act of God in your life is designed to increase, not decrease your dependence on Him. You say, "But I have talent. I can do a lot of things!" Yes, but you can do nothing that matters in God's eyes. So, before you begin your day, kneel and pray, "Lord, I'm counting on You, and I don't have a backup plan!"

PRAYER

Father, I acknowledge today that without You I can do nothing, but there are times when I try to fix things by myself and leave You out of the picture. You want me to be totally dependent on You. So, by an act of my will I choose to put everything into Your hands today.

_____
_____
_____
_____

GOD'S PART

Lord, I know that I can't do Your part, and You won't do mine. So I trust you to:

_____
_____
_____
_____

MY PART

_____
_____
_____
_____

You don't want me to carry my burdens alone, because You are my burden-bearer, my way-maker, and Your love for me never fails. And that's how I know, that of all the people in my life, You love me most!

KEEPING A GRATEFUL ATTITUDE

82

GIVE THANKS

"In everything give thanks."

1 THESSALONIANS 5:18 NKJV

*G*ratitude works like a vaccine: it keeps you from getting infected with a spirit of "grumpiness." It's the antitoxin that counteracts the poisonous effects of ingratitude. Have you noticed that we live in a thankless society? Paul said, "In the last days...people will be self-centered...and ungrateful (2 Timothy 31-2 AMPC). This generation lacks godly principles; they haven't been taught to pray at home or at school. Because they've witnessed the fall of high-profile church leaders, they've concluded that "religion" doesn't work. But thanklessness is a problem among Christians too. We ask God for things, then when we get them, we complain about having to take care of them! Ever do that? If you want to know God's will, listen: "In everything give thanks, for this is the will of God" (1 Thessalonians 5:18 NKJV). We're supposed to demonstrate thankfulness. Paul says, "With thanksgiving, let your requests be made known" (Philippians 4:6 NKJV). Why? Because thanksgiving moves them through God's approval process. It also demonstrates that you are mature enough to handle whatever He sends. After all, why would He send more if you don't appreciate what you already have? Sometimes thanksgiving is a sacrifice. It's easy to give thanks when you feel good. It's when you don't that it becomes a sacrifice made in obedience to God's Word. David said, "I will offer...the sacrifice of thanksgiving and...call on the... Lord" (Psalm 116:17 AMPC). Notice: he only called on God after he'd offered the sacrifice of thanksgiving. Your flesh will always find reasons to be dissatisfied. Your spirit will always search for reasons to be thankful. So today—be thankful!

PRAYER

Lord, help me remember to always be grateful for everything You have done in my life. Today I stop and say THANK YOU for the many times You have rescued me and provided for me. You are a good God and I have so many blessings to thank You for right now.

_____
_____
_____
_____

GOD'S PART

Lord, I know that I can't do Your part, and You won't do mine. So I trust you to:

_____
_____
_____
_____

MY PART

_____
_____
_____
_____

I read in Your Word that Your mercies are new every morning, and great is Your faithfulness. You have been faithful to me all my life. And that's how I know, that of all the people in my life, You love me most!

83

LOOK FOR THINGS TO BE GRATEFUL FOR

"Blessed be the Lord, who daily loads us with benefits."

PSALM 68:19 NKJV

The story is told of a twelve-year-old boy who had never spoken a word in his life. As a result, his parents thought he couldn't speak. Then one day his mother placed a bowl of soup in front of him and he took a spoonful. He pushed it away and said, "This is awful; I won't eat it!" The family was ecstatic. His father said, "Why haven't you ever talked to us before?" The boy replied, "Because up until now everything's been okay." The only time some of us speak is to complain! You say, "But I've got nothing to be grateful for." Really? If you slept eight hours last night, there are millions of insomniacs who would gladly switch places with you. If you have a job, a roof over your head, and three-square meals a day, there are millions of unemployed people who would like to have your problem. If you were able to get out of bed this morning and move through the day pain free, you're blessed with the gift of health. Without it, you would truly have something to complain about! And what about your salvation? What price would you put on that? Your sins have been forgiven, you have peace with God, and when you die you have a home in heaven. Sure, we all have trials and tough days. But don't insult God and belittle His blessings by saying you don't have anything to be grateful for. It's time you started talking to yourself, as David the psalmist did: "Bless the Lord, O my soul, and forget not all his benefits" (Psalm 103:2 NKJV).

PRAYER
Father, even on the rough days, I know I need to remind myself to be grateful and say thank you for all You have done for me. I get so caught up in myself sometimes that I forget. You are my source, everything I have comes from You. Thank you.

_____
_____
_____
_____

GOD'S PART
Lord, I know that I can't do Your part, and You won't do mine. So I trust you to:

_____
_____
_____
_____

MY PART

_____
_____
_____
_____

211

My life is filled with blessings and I can't count the times You have rescued me and helped me get back on my feet again. And that's how I know, that of all the people in my life, You love me most!

84

THINGS CHANGE, BUT GOD DOESN'T!

"Find enjoyment in...all the days which God gives."

ECCLESIASTES 5:18 AMPC

*O*ver one hundred times in Scripture we read, "It came to pass." That's because most things in life aren't permanent. Things change, but God doesn't! Knowing that can help you to handle the bad times and stop you from clinging so tightly to the good ones. Here are three important truths to keep in mind: (1) Enjoy today. It's a gift—that's why it's called "the present." Solomon said, "To enjoy your work and accept your lot in life— this is indeed a gift from God" (Ecclesiastes 5:19 NLT). Even though you are constantly moving toward another goal or objective, learn to live in the present. Don't put your joy on hold, or let it slip away while you're waiting for the next big event. (2) Learn to appreciate the little things. They're all around you: the love of a good friend, a kind deed, a fresh insight, a good night's sleep, the delight on your child's face. When you appreciate what you have, it multiplies. When you're grateful for the little things, God will give you more to appreciate (See Matthew 25:23 KJV). (3) Each ending brings a new beginning. There are two myths you should never believe. The first is the "forever myth," which says your situation will never improve. The second is the "never myth," which says if things get any worse, you'll never be able to handle them. Both are distortions. God's Word says everything comes "to pass." And while you're going through it, He promises to "strengthen...and help you" (Isaiah 41:10 NIV). Yes, this ending will bring your new beginning. So, keep trusting God.

PRAYER

Lord, I know that each day is a gift from You, and I need to enjoy it to the fullest. Help me to live in the present and not get ahead of You. To focus on what you are doing in my life today, not what I want You to do tomorrow and to appreciate the little things in life.

_____
_____
_____
_____

GOD'S PART

Lord, I know that I can't do Your part, and You won't do mine. So I trust you to:

_____
_____
_____
_____

MY PART

_____
_____
_____
_____

213

Each day I awaken I see Your hand of blessing and Your provision all around me. You are present in every detail of my life. And that's how I know, that of all the people in my life, You love me most!

85

BE GRATEFUL FOR
YOUR BLESSINGS

"I went away full, but the Lord has brought me back empty."

RUTH 1:21 NIV

When it comes to valuable life-lessons, the book of Ruth tops the best-seller list. (Have you read it yet?) When famine came to Bethlehem, Naomi, her husband and two sons moved to Moab where the economy was thriving. What they hoped would be a short stay turned into ten years. Their sons married two local girls, Ruth and Orpah. Then the unthinkable happened. Naomi's husband and sons died. As a result of her loss she became bitter. When she heard that times were good in Bethlehem she decided to go back home. After she arrived, she said, "I went out full, and the Lord has brought me home again empty" (Ruth 1:21 NKJV). What did she mean? She was saying that despite the famine at home in Bethlehem, at least there she had her husband and sons, whereas in Moab, "the land of plenty," she'd lost them. You never miss the water till the well runs dry! The truth is, you can be blessed and not know it. Only as you look back do you realize that what you have, is much more important than all the things you don't have. When Naomi lost what she loved most, even a famine seemed insignificant by comparison. Have you been saying, "I'll be happy when…"? No, happiness doesn't come from getting what you want, it comes from appreciating what God's given you. Instead of whining and complaining about your lot in life, stop and ask yourself, "What would I take in exchange for what I have?" If you don't know the answer, begin counting your blessings and thanking God for them.

PRAYER

Lord, on the days when I spend too much time whining and complaining, stop me in my tracks, and remind me of all you have done for me. I never want to be ungrateful or go through life with a glass half empty attitude. Gratitude should always be at the center of my life.

_____

_____

_____

_____

GOD'S PART

Lord, I know that I can't do Your part, and You won't do mine. So I trust you to:

_____

_____

_____

_____

MY PART

_____

_____

_____

_____

My life is filled to the brim with all the good things You have given to me and the ways You have provided for me and my family. And that's how I know, that of all the people in my life, You love me most!

86

DON'T FORGET TO THANK GOD

"When you have eaten and are satisfied,
praise the Lord your God."

DEUTERONOMY 8:10 NIV

*W*e decided to reprint this story because its message is timeless. "They huddled inside the storm door—two children in ragged, oversized coats. 'Any old papers, lady?' I was busy. I wanted to say no—until I saw their feet. Little sandals sopped with sleet. 'Come in and I'll make you some hot cocoa.' There was no conversation. Their soggy sandals left marks on the hearthstone. I served them cocoa with toast and jam to fortify them against the chill outside. Then I went back to the kitchen to work on my household budget. The silence in the front room struck through me. I looked in. The little girl held the empty cup in her hands and looked at it. The boy asked, 'Lady, are you rich?' I looked at my shabby slipcovers. 'Am I rich? Mercy, no!' The girl put the cup in its saucer—carefully. 'Your cups match your saucers.' Her voice was old with a hunger not of the stomach. They then left, holding their bundles of paper against the wind. They hadn't said thank you. They didn't need to—they'd done more than that. Much more. Plain blue pottery cups and saucers, but they matched. Potatoes in brown gravy; a roof over our heads; my man with a good steady job—these things matched, too. I moved the chairs back from the fire and tidied the living room. The muddy prints of small sandals were still wet on my hearth. I let them be. I want them there in case I ever forget how rich I am!" The word for you today is: Don't forget to thank God.

PRAYER

Father, today my prayer is simply this: thank you for being my friend, thank you for forgiving all my sins, thank you for my job, my family, my health, my home, and my children. I am truly over-whelmed with gratitude for all You have done for me. THANK YOU!

_____
_____
_____
_____

GOD'S PART

Lord, I know that I can't do Your part, and You won't do mine. So I trust you to:

_____
_____
_____
_____

MY PART

_____
_____
_____
_____

217

When I stop and see You in the everyday things of life and look at the beauty all around me in creation, I know without a doubt, that of all the people in my life, You love me most!

THE PRAYER OF FAITH

87

HOW TO ACTIVATE
GOD'S WORD (1)

"Let Christ's word with all it's wisdom...live in you."

COLOSSIANS 3:16 GWT

*M*aking the right decisions and choosing the right actions are the crux of living successfully. If you are the source of your own wisdom, or you're looking to others, your odds are not good. Paul writes, "Let Christ's word with all its wisdom and richness live in you" (Colossians 3:16 NLT). If you do, you'll have the winning strategy for your life. But you must: (1) Read it. You don't have to understand it all; it's not an intellectual exercise. Reading it prayerfully brings power and wisdom because "the Word that God speaks is alive and active...[penetrating] to the place where soul and spirit meet" (Hebrews 4:12 PHPS). (2) Meditate on it. That means "chew on" it. Let your spiritual digestive juices process God's Word until its nutrients become part of you: strengthening, energizing, and directing you. (3) Believe it. "My word... always produces...It will accomplish all I want it to" (Isaiah 55:11 NKJV). There's only one thing that can short-circuit God's Word—unbelief. "The message...did them no good, because they only heard and did not believe as well" (Hebrews 4:2 PHPS). "Hearing" opens the door; "believing" walks through it and activates the promise. (4) Receive it. No matter how strongly you believe in God's promises and His intention to give them to you, they're not yours until you receive them by faith. "Therefore I tell you, whatever you ask for in prayer, believe that you have received it, and it will be yours" (Mark 11:24 NIV). So, believe your answer is on the way, and keep your faith strong until it arrives.

PRAYER
Lord, I now understand that in order to get my prayers answered I must know what Your Word says about my circumstances. The thing that most often stands in my way is unbelief. The more I meditate on Your Word, the stronger my faith becomes, and I have confidence that You will meet my needs.

_____
_____
_____
_____

GOD'S PART
Lord, I know that I can't do Your part, and You won't do mine. So I trust you to:

_____
_____
_____
_____

MY PART

_____
_____
_____
_____

The Word of God is alive, it has the power to change my life, break every chain, heal my body, and renew and restore my mind. And that's how I know, that of all the people in my life, You love me most!

88

HOW TO ACTIVATE
GOD'S WORD (2)

"If we ask anything according to his will, he hears us."

1 JOHN 5:14 NIV

*W*hile you are waiting for God's Word to be fulfilled in your life, do these three things: (1) Verbalize it. The most effective way to pray is to speak God's Word. The patriarchs, prophets, and psalmists regularly reminded God of His promises in prayer, confident He would keep them. The surest indicator of God's will is His Word. "This is the confidence we have in approaching God: that if we ask anything according to his will, he hears us. And if we know that he hears us...we know that we have what we asked of him" (1 John 5:14-15 NIV). God always responds to His Word, always! (2) Obey it. God's plan for us is not just to speak His Word, vital as this is—but that we obey it (See James 1:22 NIV). The hymn writer said: "When we walk with the Lord in the light of His Word, what a glory He sheds on our way; while we do His good will, He abides with us still, and with all who will trust and obey." Obedience—faith in action—aligns us with God and He responds by fulfilling His promise to us. (3) Share it. Parents and grandparents, "Take to heart these words that I give you today. Repeat them to your children. Talk about them when you're at home or away, when you lie down or get up" (Deuteronomy 6:6-7 GWT). You needn't be a qualified teacher, just a sincere teller. Sharing God's Word will produce fruit in the lives of your family, friends, relatives, business associates, and neighbors, and increase your own grasp and understanding of it.

PRAYER
Lord, I am so glad that I decided to commit to spending time with You in prayer each day. I have learned so much about Your Word and how it will work in my life—if I work it. I have already experienced my prayers being answered because I took the time to declare Your Word over my circumstances.

_____
_____
_____
_____

GOD'S PART
Lord, I know that I can't do Your part, and You won't do mine. So I trust you to:

_____
_____
_____
_____

MY PART

_____
_____
_____
_____

I am learning to embrace Your will for my life. I am fighting less and accepting more. I am asking less and praising more. And that's how I know, that of all the people in my life, You love me most!

89

"I'M PRAYING FOR YOU"

"I have prayed for you."

LUKE 22:32 NKJV

*W*hen somebody says, "I'm praying for you," there is no greater expression of love! The tragedy of religion without power is that it leaves you ignorant of the incredible potential of prayer. Prayer moves God! And when God moves, people and situations change! Jesus told Peter, "Satan has asked for you, that he may sift you as wheat. But I have prayed for you, that your faith should not fail; and when you have returned to Me, strengthen your brethren" (Luke 22:31-32 NKJV). And God answered that prayer! In spite of his denial of Christ, Peter ended up leading one of the greatest spiritual awakenings in history, and two of the books in the Bible are named after him. Only eternity will reveal the lives that have been salvaged and ministries restored through prayer. There is no distance in prayer. Through prayer you can project yourself into any situation, at anytime, anywhere on earth, claiming the promise, "Whatever you ask for in prayer, believe that you have received it, and it will be yours" (Mark 11:24 NIV). When the Philistines were about to annihilate Israel, Samuel said, "I will intercede with the Lord for you" (1 Samuel 7:5 NIV). And the result? "The Lord thun-dered...against the Philistines" (1 Samuel 7:10 NIV). Perhaps this is what the old-timers meant when they talked about "prayin' up a storm!" God comes by invitation. Your prayers open the door to Him. Any time you pray in Jesus' name, the Holy Spirit is authorized to go to work accomplishing things on your behalf that cannot be accomplished any other way. Remember that, next time someone says, "I'm praying for you."

PRAYER

Lord, I am grateful for those times when I had someone pray for me when I couldn't pray for myself. Without their prayers I probably wouldn't have made it. I commit today to not just saying the words, "I'm praying for you" but to following through on that promise when someone shares a need with me.

_____

_____

_____

_____

GOD'S PART

Lord, I know that I can't do Your part, and You won't do mine. So I trust you to:

_____

_____

_____

_____

MY PART

_____

_____

_____

_____

> Nothing is more powerful than prayer. Only prayer can make a way where there seems to be no way. Only prayer can turn the darkness into light. And that's how I know, that of all the people in my life, You love me most!

90

KEEP PRAYING AND BELIEVING

"Teaching them more about prayer, he used [a] story."

LUKE 11:5 NLT

*Y*our need moves God's heart, but your faith moves Him to action. So, keep praying and believing. Jesus gives us two illustrations of this: (1) "Suppose you went to a friend's house at midnight, wanting to borrow three loaves...he calls out from his bedroom, 'Don't bother me. The door is locked for the night, and [we] are all in bed. I can't help you.' But I tell you this—though he won't do it for friendship's sake, if you keep knocking long enough, he will get up and give you whatever you need because of your shameless persistence" (Luke 11:5-8 NLT). Why will God answer your prayer? To protect His reputation as One who makes covenants and keeps them. (2) "There was a judge in a certain city...A widow of that city came to him repeatedly, saying, 'Give me justice'...The judge ignored her for a while, but finally he said...'I don't fear God or care about people, but this woman is driving me crazy. I'm going to see that she gets justice, because she is wearing me out with her constant requests!' Then the Lord said, 'Learn a lesson from this unjust judge. Even he rendered a just decision in the end. So, don't you think God will surely give justice to his chosen people who cry out to him day and night? Will he keep putting them off? I tell you, he will grant justice to them quickly'" (Luke 18:2-8 NLT). Bottom line: The God you serve is just, compassionate, able, and willing to meet your needs, so keep praying and believing.

PRAYER

Lord, so much has changed since I've been on this prayer journey with You. I have learned to pray in faith according to Your Word, to be persistent and not give up hope because the answer doesn't come when I think it should. Most of all, I've learned that prayer isn't just about asking You for things, it's about how prayer chang-es me and allows me to see things through Your eyes.

_____
_____
_____
_____

GOD'S PART

Lord, I know that I can't do Your part, and You won't do mine. So I trust you to:

_____
_____
_____
_____

MY PART

_____
_____
_____
_____

I don't ever want to go back to a prayerless life. I want to stay connected to You. I no longer have to be anxious or afraid. And that's how I know, that of all the people in my life, You love me most!

91

THE PRAYER OF FAITH

"The prayer of faith shall save the sick."

JAMES 5:15

When a pastor visited a lady in a nursing home, she asked him to pray for her healing. So, he did. Then she said, "Would you help me out of this wheelchair?" Startled, he complied. She took a few steps then started running and jumping till the whole building heard her. Later in his car the pastor looked up and said, "Lord, don't ever do that to me again!" The Bible says, "The prayer of faith shall save the sick." So why are we surprised when He does? A visiting preacher told the congregation if anyone needed prayer to come forward, though inwardly he was thinking about his past lack of results. Thirty people responded and he prayed for them. Later that week a woman called and said, "Last Sunday you prayed for my husband. He had cancer, and he died." "Much good my prayers did," he thought. The lady continued, "When we walked into church my husband was angry. He wanted to see his grandchildren grow up, and every day he cursed God. Being around him was unbearable. But after you prayed for him, he walked out a different person. His last days were the best we'd ever had; we talked, laughed, and sang hymns together. He wasn't cured, but he was healed." Only God knows why some are healed while others aren't. But our instructions are clear. "Is any sick among you? Let him call for the elders of the church; and let them pray over him, anointing him with oil in the name of the Lord: And the prayer of faith shall save the sick, and the Lord shall raise him up" (James 5:14-15 NKJV).

PRAYER

"Is anyone among you sick? He must call for the elders (spiritual leaders) of the church and they are to pray over him, anointing him with oil in the name of the Lord; and the prayer of faith will restore the one who is sick, and the Lord will raise him up" (James 5:14-15 AMP).

_____
_____
_____
_____

GOD'S PART

Lord, I know that I can't do Your part, and You won't do mine. So I trust you to:

_____
_____
_____
_____

MY PART

_____
_____
_____
_____

Nothing is impossible to those who believe. There is no problem that You can't solve or any sickness that You can't heal. You are Jehovah Rapha—the God who heals. And that's how I know, that of all the people in my life, You love me most!

ACKNOWLEDGMENTS

Page 30 - Making Prayer A Priority
Hughes, R. Kent. Disciplines of a Godly Man. (Wheaton, IL: Crossway, 1991). 105.

Page 46 - You Must Exercise Faith
Roberts, Mark D. "Amazing Unbelief." Posted November 16, 2009.

Page 80 - What To Do In A Crisis
Warren, Rick. God's Answers to Life's Difficult Questions. (Grand Rapids, MI: Zondervan, 2006). 126-127.

Page 180 - Take Control of Your Life
Maxwell, John C. Put Your Dream to the Test. (Nashville, TN: Thomas Nelson, 2009). 15.

Page 130 - Are You Struggling Financially?
Bible Prayers for All Your Needs. Victory House (Tulsa, OK: Victory House, 1999). 264-275.

Page 140 - Standing on His Promise
Dr. Ben Carson, Neurosurgeon, Brain Stem
Carson, Benjamin S., M.D. "Standing on God's Promise." www.guideposts.com. (Accessed February 19, 2009.)

Page 146 - Now Faith
Walker, Jon. "Can You See It?" Accessed September 30, 2009. www.gracecreates.com.

Page 178 - Does This Person Belong In My Life?
Jakes, T. D. Before You Do. (New York: Atria Books, 2008).

Page 192 - Forgiveness
Armstrong, Kristin. Work in Progress. (Brentwood, TN: FaithWords, 2009).

JOURNEY NOTES

JOURNEY NOTES

JOURNEY NOTES

JOURNEY NOTES

JOURNEY NOTES

JOURNEY NOTES

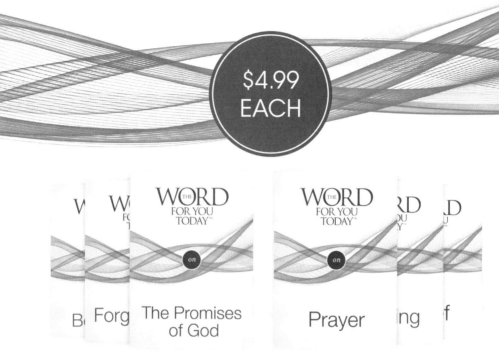